To one who knows what it
means!

With best wishes

Betty Wason

DINNERS THAT WAIT

BOOKS BY BETTY WASON

Dinners That Wait
Miracle in Hellas: *The Greeks Fight On*
Cooking Without Cans

DINNERS THAT WAIT:

A Cookbook by BETTY WASON

With line drawings by Margot Tomes

Doubleday & Company, Inc., Garden City, New York, 1954

LIBRARY OF CONGRESS CATALOG CARD NUMBER 54–7665

Copyright, 1954, by Elizabeth Wason Hall
All Rights Reserved
Printed in the United States at
The Country Life Press, Garden City, N.Y.
First Edition

Designed by Diana Klemin

Contents

Introduction

There's nothing more pleasurable than having people in to dinner. At least, that's the way I feel about it. I like to cook, and I like to watch the smile of delight that comes over the faces of my guests as they taste well-prepared food. And I've always noticed that the best conversation of all grows out of the mellow atmosphere of a happy dinner table.

The first requisite of a good cook is true enjoyment of food. Anyone who really loves to eat can easily learn to cook. However, I've known cooking fools, who produce their culinary triumphs with as much éclat as if they were actors taking a curtain call, yet create so much turmoil in the process that their guests are both famished and dizzy with the clatter before the food appears.

Dinner is always more fun for me if I can sit down with my guests to enjoy a leisurely cocktail before serving the meal. They seem to enjoy it more, too, if the process of putting the meal together is smoothly under control.

Every menu offered in this book is intended for a company dinner. Any of them, of course, can be served at home on an ordinary night. But it seems to me most people like to serve something special when guests are due, so with this in mind, I've suggested how the hostess can manage to be in the living room during the first round of cocktails and not have to worry about the dinner spoiling. Each main dish is delay-proof. Either it (1) is in the oven baking, or on the top of the stove simmering when guests arrive, and a few minutes' extra cooking time doesn't matter, (2) it can be prepared hours beforehand, then heated up in a sauce or with some other added flourish at the last minute, or (3) the dish requires no more than fifteen or twenty minutes' cooking time, so it can be put on the stove after the guests are beginning to feel mellow.

Perhaps most important of all, from the cook's viewpoint, these menus won't be ruined if the guests are an hour late arriving. It's a heartbreaking thing to see a good meal dry up to leather because of people who don't yet know how to tell time. This could even apply to husbands.

One word of warning. I'm a taste-testing cook, and though I've tried hard to capture exact measurements in each of the recipes offered in this book, I have to confess that my usual method is to keep on adding things until the final product tastes as I think it should. I recommend the method. This is heresy, I know, to the adherents of scientific cookery. I was trained as a home economist myself. But I like to think of cooking as more art than science. In fact, I not only urge taste-testing, I suggest you use daring and imagination in altering the recipes that follow. Once when preparing broilers to be baked with white grapes and dry white wine, I reached for the wine bottle only to find it empty, so I used sweet vermouth instead—and discovered an entirely new and delicious dish. Often the most spectacular successes in cooking happen through just such accidents.

There is further reason for tasting as you go along. Ingredients vary greatly in strength and flavor. Garlic, for example, is so strong during certain seasons that one clove may be as potent as three at another time. Herbs and spices also vary according to age, degree of dryness, and other factors. Even salt varies in its saltiness. Some tomatoes contain far more water than others. And the brand of canned consommé you use as beef stock may be so strong with artificial flavoring you'll have to add half a dozen other things to disguise it.

Then, too, the best of cooks occasionally get absent-minded. You might have left out some vital ingredient.

Most of mine are exotic recipes, because that's the kind I happen to like best. Many I learned while wandering around Europe as a foreign correspondent. However, I enjoyed foreign food long before I set foot on foreign shores, and I have become acquainted with many exotic dishes in the gourmet world of New York City.

In a way I dislike the word "gourmet." It's so snobbish. I have never been able to understand why a recipe must be "authentic" as long as it's good. The important thing, as I see it, is to approach mealtime with eagerness and lack of prejudice. Any food that is well prepared, properly seasoned, and served with joy merits respect.

It is with this spirit I offer the recipes which follow.

Efficiency is important in any venture, even in art. Efficiency is absolutely essential in meal planning.

The best way to plan a company dinner is to sit with paper and pencil for as long as necessary, jotting down every item that is needed for the meal, and arranging a work schedule so that each step can be completed in its own time. This may sound like a lot of trouble. Actually, it saves trouble, for in this way one avoids having several tasks demanding attention at the same time, with the risk of ruining good food.

Some of the recipes in this collection may look complicated. However, if you examine them more closely, you'll find the same seasonings pop up again and again. A well-stocked herb and spice shelf is the answer. The initial cost may run to several dollars, but the herbs last a long time, and the cost per meal is infinitesimal.

In my own kitchen, I find the following condiments most important: oregano, thyme, basil, bay leaves, mace, nutmeg, curry powder, paprika, cinnamon, mustard (both dry and prepared), and horseradish. Next in importance come chili powder, tarragon, dill, marjoram, ginger root, sage, dried hot red pepper, tabasco sauce, and Worcestershire sauce.

Then there is wine, so necessary for lifting plain food into the "something special" class. I quarrel with those who urge the use of expensive wines. The cheaper brands of domestic wine will do very nicely. This is especially true of sherry, the most useful of all wines for cooking in my estimation. Sherry adds zest to sauces, stews, desserts, and chilled fruit mixtures. Port is good for certain meats, but generally speaking the dry red wine is preferable in recipes calling for red wine. The acid of the wine helps to tenderize meat. The same is true of dry white wine, of course. Lamb for shashlyk, for example, is best marinated in a Rhine type along with herbs, garlic, lemon juice, and olive oil.

Vermouth can be used in a number of ways. Brandy is important not only for certain desserts, but in some meat dishes, too. Rum is fine for flaming. By the time you reach the last chapter in this book, if you're still with me, you'll probably have such a good cellar in your pantry, to coin a phrase, it will be easy to pick and choose—and set your imagination to work making new creations of your own.

A touch of spirits helps to soothe the waiting dinner quite as much as the guests on the other side of the wall.

And what about the spirits to be served the guests who have come for dinner? In the menus that follow there is continual reference to cocktails, yet I have not suggested specific drinks for specific meals. The reason is that I've found most people prefer the traditional old stand-bys: highballs, martinis, manhattans, Scotch and soda. Those who abstain from alcoholic drinks will stick by tomato juice, fruit juice, or one of the carbonated beverages.

Fancy concoctions are not likely to win you new friends. People may politely accept the queer cocktail and tell you they like it, but after they've gone home there may be unkind words.

Few of us can afford to offer the entire gamut of whiskeys, and if we did, there would probably be someone asking for another brand than those offered. You can't please everyone in this respect, so don't try.

For a small gathering, I find it works out pretty well to offer martinis and either rye or bourbon highballs. Scotch drinkers usually will settle for a martini, though they turn up their noses at any other kind of whiskey. Bourbon drinkers will settle for rye, and vice versa. If you can afford to offer Scotch as well, you will come close to pleasing them all.

For a larger crowd, manhattans and martinis are easiest, though probably you had better have at least one bottle of a whiskey tucked away for those persnickety individuals who won't touch anything but a straight drink. For a large number of guests cocktails are far easier to serve than highballs, and do not require nearly as much ice. You can mix extra quantities of both manhattans and martinis ahead of time, and store them in milk bottles in the refrigerator, if you're afraid one cocktail shaker of each will not be enough.

As for the proportions to use in mixing martinis and manhattans— that I leave to you. There are those who make martinis with 7 parts gin to 1 part vermouth. That I find absolutely poisonous. The standard, old-fashioned recipe is 3 parts gin to 1 of vermouth. When, in more intimate gatherings I mix a private cocktail for myself, I often reverse the proportions, fill the glass nearly full with dry vermouth, then add a little gin. They do this in Paris. But whether it would find favor with many Americans is questionable.

Many people now like "dry manhattans," made of two parts rye to one part dry vermouth, with a twist of lemon peel instead of a maraschino cherry. Then there are "Rob Roys," made of Scotch and dry vermouth. And whiskey sours, and daiquiris, and Tom Collins, all of which have their own following. But be sure of your company before you serve any of these.

In warm weather a Tom Collins before dinner will please most people, even those who do not touch gin in any form during the winter. Rum Collins with lemon, sugar, and soda is another drink welcomed by many in hot weather, though rum is risky among regular whiskey drinkers.

If old friends are coming, and you know them to be open-minded when it comes to mixed drinks, you might branch out with a lesser known cocktail, or even one of your own invention. Once, for a summer affair, I served cocktails made with 3 jiggers of rum to 1 of Cointreau and half a jigger of lemon juice (no sugar). Another mixture that many people seem to like is a sort of cross between whiskey sour and dry manhattan: rye whiskey, lemon juice, sugar, and dry vermouth. Experiment with these if you want to be different, but only on people you know well.

Wine and soda makes a good after-dinner long drink in hot weather, but it's not, in my opinion, suitable for a before-dinner drink. If it's to be wine before dinner, dry white wine, or cocktail dry sherry, or vermouth are the best bets.

For those who do not drink alcoholic beverages, tomato juice, Coca-Cola, ginger ale, frozen orange juice, or frozen lemonade all qualify as good aperitifs.

But whether the cocktail is made of tomato juice or of gin and vermouth, the custom of offering a drink to guests as soon as they arrive is a gracious one. Basically the idea is the same as that behind the ancient loving cup. It's a way of saying welcome.

One final word about the menus that follow. They are complete menus, every one, and the directions are given accordingly. But suppose you don't want to follow the menu as given? You may have a favorite dessert you want to substitute, or the vegetable suggested may not be in season, or you simply like to do things your own way.

Go right ahead! That's your privilege. If you don't like the dessert suggested for a particular menu, turn to the index, and you'll find over sixty others listed. The same flexibility holds true where numbers are suggested. Most menus planned for 6 persons can be enlarged for 8 or 10, or one planned for 10 can be reduced to do for 6. In many cases I've suggested how.

There are several reasons why these have been arranged as complete menus, instead of the recipes being listed in the traditional way. For one thing, the menu directions demonstrate a system of preparation, showing you how to have everything under control, no matter how long dinner may be delayed. For another thing, desserts suitable and easy for a large dinner party are combined with main courses planned for a large number, and vice versa. And finally, here are flavor and texture combinations that complement each other nicely. Nevertheless, these are not intended as hard-and-fast combinations. In fact, anticipating that many if not most cooks will want to do things their own way, I've been careful to keep each recipe intact, so that if you're using just one recipe out of the menu, and everything else in the meal is your own, you will still find the directions useful. Good hunting!

You will be able to locate all those recipes which are capitalized in the text by consulting the index.

DINNERS THAT WAIT

Let the Soup Simmer

MENU

Cocktail Appetizers
Lentil Soup with Ham and Cheese
Green Salad
Fruit, Cheese, Cookies   Coffee

FOR EIGHT

This is a hearty, rich soup, excellent for a cold winter's eve. Serve it to friends who like highly seasoned food. Improves in flavor if prepared a day ahead and reheated shortly before guests are due.

STEP 1: Two days in advance, cover 2 cups lentils with water. Soak overnight.

STEP 2: A day ahead, make

LENTIL SOUP

Remnants of baked ham, including bone
1 large or 2 small onions, sliced
2 or 3 cloves garlic, minced
3 tablespoons fat or drippings
1½ teaspoons salt
½ teaspoon marjoram
2 cups lentils, soaked
½ cup coarsely grated Swiss cheese
Vienna or French type bread

Brown onion and garlic in heated fat in large heavy kettle or pressure cooker. Add soaked, drained lentils, 3 quarts cold water, marjoram, and salt. Add ham bone, along with any scraps of ham left from roast. Cover. Simmer for 2 hours, or until lentils are tender. Taste. Since ham varies greatly in saltiness, it's hard to give an exact measurement of salt needed. You may want more. Cool. Place in refrigerator.

If prepared in pressure cooker, follow cooking instructions for any bean soup.

To serve 4 people, cut recipe in half, but be sure to taste for salt. Proportionately a little more salt may be necessary, unless the ham is quite salty.

STEP 3: Prepare cocktail appetizers, so that your guests will have something to nibble on during the 15 or 20 minutes required for you to put the meal together. Here is a suggestion:

CURRIED
TUNA FISH CANAPÉS

2 cloves garlic
½ cup tuna fish
2 tablespoons horse-radish
3 stalks celery, finely chopped
1 teaspoon curry powder
¼ cup mayonnaise
Few drops lemon juice
¼ teaspoon salt

Mash the garlic to a pulp in a mixing bowl. Throw out any shreds that may be left. Then add remaining ingredients. Taste. You may want a little more salt and mayonnaise. To serve, place the bowl containing the tuna fish in the center of a platter, surrounded by crackers, and let people make their own canapés.

If you want another tidbit to accompany cocktails, cheese popcorn would be good.

STEP 4: Rub salad bowl with garlic (see above). Add salad greens which have been thoroughly washed and cut into serving pieces. Place bowl in refrigerator. Mix salad dressing separately, or arrange condiments, oil, and vinegar on table to mix at *table* when the time comes.

Here is a good, simple

FRENCH DRESSING	½ teaspoon salt
	Pinch curry powder, or
	¼ teaspoon savory salt
	½ teaspoon dry mustard
	½ to ¾ tablespoon vinegar
	1½ to 2 tablespoons olive oil or
	salad oil

Add salt, curry powder, and mustard to salad spoon. Dissolve with vinegar. Toss salad greens with this. Then add oil, using your own taste to determine how much. Some olive oils are much stronger in flavor than others, and consequently less will be required. This makes enough dressing for quite a large bowl of salad.

STEP 5: An hour before guests are due, arrange mixed fruit in bowl. Chill in refrigerator. Arrange assorted cheese and crackers or bread on serving platter. Place cookies in bowl.

STEP 6: Set table. Put coffee and water in pot. Arrange cocktail appetizers in bowls in living room. Get dressed. Relax.

STEP 7: Shortly before guests are due, slice bread thick, toast lightly under broiler. Place a slice of toast in each soup dish. Top with coarsely grated Swiss cheese. Take chilled lentils from refrigerator and reheat. Add more water if the soup seems very thick. Leave soup barely simmering on stove until guests have all arrived and conversation is mellow. You should be mellow and relaxed then, too, since there are no feverish last-minute steps to worry you.

MENU

Cocktail Appetizers
Onion Soup
Chef's Salad   Hot Rolls
Apple Dumplings   Coffee

FOR SIX

Light but substantial. Good Sunday-night fare.

STEP 1: Preceding day, make

ONION SOUP

2 quarts soup stock, from
   2 pounds chicken necks
1½ teaspoons salt
1 cup thinly sliced onions
3 tablespoons butter
1 tablespoon flour
French bread, toasted
Parmesan cheese

Cover chicken necks with cold water, add salt. Bring slowly to boil. Turn heat low, simmer, tightly covered, for 2 hours (or prepare in pressure cooker). Cool. Strain, removing chicken necks. Pour this stock into quart jars or milk bottles and place in refrigerator. Fat will rise to top and coagulate so that it can be easily removed.

When stock has been clarified, brown onions in butter. Add flour, blending carefully. Gradually add stock. If necessary, add water to stock to make 2 quarts. Bring to boil. Simmer 1 hour. Taste to make sure it has the right amount of salt. Put in refrigerator until 1 hour before you expect to serve dinner.

STEP 2: While soup simmers, prepare

APPLE DUMPLINGS

6 medium cooking apples
2 tablespoons butter
½ teaspoon cinnamon
¾ cup sugar
Pastry
½ cup raisins

Make pie crust dough in your favorite way, using 3 cups of flour.

Cut into 6 portions, for easier handling. Roll out thin. Cut into squares large enough to wrap each apple completely. Pare and core each apple before placing it in the center of a pastry square. Fill cavity of each apple with raisins, sugar and cinnamon blended together. (Both cinnamon and raisins are optional. If you are a person of simple tastes, sugar alone may go into the cavity.) Dot with butter. To fold pastry, moisten edges with cold water, press edges together with tines of a fork, then flute so that each dumpling looks flowerlike. Prick completed dumpling all over with a fork. Bake in hot oven, 400°F., for 30 minutes, or until golden brown. May be served plain or with lemon or wine sauce.

STEP 3: While dumplings are in oven, start fixing cocktail appetizers. A good choice with this meal: potato chips, peanuts, and

AVOCADO-BACON	2 ripe avocados
CANAPÉS	1 tablespoon lemon juice
	1 tablespoon onion juice, or
	2 cloves garlic
	½ teaspoon salt
	½ cup chopped black olives
	2 tablespoons olive oil
	2 slices bacon, minced

Peel and stone avocados. If using garlic, rub mixing bowl with garlic until mashed to a pulp, then throw remaining shreds away. Add avocado to this bowl, and mash to a pulp with fork. If using onion, grate onion juice into bowl over the avocado. Add lemon juice to avocado to prevent its turning black. Cook bacon until crisp, then drain and crumble into bits. Add salt, chopped olives, olive oil, and finally the bacon to the avocado mixture. To serve, place bowl containing this spread in the living room on a platter surrounded with crackers. Let people help themselves.

STEP 4: Prepare ingredients for

CHEF'S SALAD

½ pound boiled ham, cut in thin fingers

1 pound sharp cheddar cheese, cut in thin fingers

1 bunch water cress

1 medium head of romaine

1 egg, hard-boiled

2 medium tomatoes

French dressing

Wrap ham, cheese, and washed salad greens in waxed paper, or in plastic bags. Keep in refrigerator until serving time. Shortly before guests are due, peel and slice egg, quarter tomatoes. Then add all to large salad bowl which has been well rubbed with garlic. Place bowl in refrigerator until the salad course is due.

STEP 5: Set table. Set out appetizers in living room. Put coffee and water in pot. Get dressed. Relax.

STEP 6: Shortly before guests are due, toast French bread under broiler. Place a slice of toast in each soup dish. Have bowl of grated Parmesan cheese on table, to be passed around. After guests have started to arrive, reheat soup, keeping it at a simmer. Put rolls in the oven set at 250°F. to warm. Add prepared French dressing to salad. Serve when appetite dictates.

MENU

Cocktail Appetizers
Bouillabaisse
Crusty Rolls   Green Salad
Ice Cream Tarts   Coffee

FOR EIGHT

This seemingly light meal is very filling. Considerable preparation is necessary in advance, but the actual cooking time is brief. The name in French means "boil" and "stop." There are as many different recipes for Bouillabaisse as for beef stew, so don't be afraid to vary the ingredients. Only be sure that your guests are fond of sea food and have a liking for the exotic. The stew will be served in soup plates, but be sure to provide a platter in the center of the table for the "cemetery" of bones and shells. Paper napkins are called for too.

STEP 1: Shop around in the fish market for the following ingredients for

BOUILLABAISSE	3 pounds assorted fish (red perch, whitefish, haddock or cod, bass, bluefish, or what-have-you)
	3 or 4 lobster tails
	½ pound shrimp

Whole fish is preferable to fillets. However, you might ask the fish-man to fillet the fish for you, saving bones, head, and tail. Take these home to make the

COURT BOUILLON I	Fishbones, heads, and tails
	3 cups water
	½ teaspoon salt
	1 medium onion
	1 teaspoon oregano
	1 teaspoon thyme
	1 teaspoon basil
	1 cup white wine
	2 tablespoons butter

Combine all ingredients. Boil 15 minutes. Strain, saving the liquor.

Meantime, remove the shells from the uncooked shrimp, cutting out the black strip along the spine. Leave the lobster in the shells, but have the shells cracked so that the lobster tails may be broken into several pieces. (Frozen lobster tails and frozen shrimp may be used, but the fish itself must be fresh—really fresh, not 3 or 4 days old.)

Cut the fish into large serving pieces. Put into the refrigerator until dinnertime.

Now heat the following together in a large kettle:

½ cup olive oil
½ cup minced onion
2 or 3 garlic cloves, mashed
1½ cups canned tomatoes
 (or 2 large ripe tomatoes)
1 bay leaf
½ teaspoon minced parsley
Few shreds of thyme
½ teaspoon salt
Dash of black pepper
Few shreds saffron (optional)

Put this aside, too, until mealtime.

After all the guests have arrived and are enjoying cocktails, go into the kitchen and combine the fish with the tomato-herb mixture, and with the Court Bouillon. Look at your watch and boil the fish exactly 20 minutes.

STEP 2: Prepare the dessert. To make ICE CREAM TARTS, bake individual tart shells, one to a person, or buy patty shells from the bakery. To serve, place sliced, sugared bananas in the bottom of each and fill the tart shell or the patty shell with ice cream. (Or, use drained frozen raspberries or strawberries—previously thawed, of course, or any fruit preserves.)

STEP 3: Prepare salad greens. Wash thoroughly, cut into serving pieces. Place in bowl already rubbed with garlic. Leave in refrigerator until serving time. Mix French dressing.

STEP 4: Arrange cocktail appetizers. Since the main dish is complicated and requires last-minute attention, keep the appetizers simple, something you can buy ready to serve, such as Fritos, or Cheetos, or black olives, salted nuts or seeds.

STEP 5: Set table. If you want to do right by the Bouillabaisse, put white wine in the refrigerator to chill. Put coffee and water in pot. Get dressed.

STEP 6: After everyone has arrived, and conversation is sparkling, finish the Bouillabaisse. While you keep an eye on the clock, get out the salad, add the prepared dressing to it. Place sliced bananas, or other fruit, in the tart or patty shells. Fill glasses with chilled wine. You can see to all these last-minute details in the 20 minutes required for cooking the fish. Then call everyone to the table and have fun.

MENU

Cocktail Appetizers
Borscht   *Assorted Piroshki*
Fig-Apricot-Raspberry Compote   **Coffee**

FOR EIGHT

Borscht is to the Russians and Poles what minestrone is to the Italians, what pot-au-feu is to the French. Anything and everything may be added. The one distinguishing characteristic is its red color. Generally this comes from beets, but it can be supplied by red cabbage. The red cabbage liquid turns to an ugly purple when heated, so if your Borscht should be made with a cabbage rather than beet base, serve it cold—the color then is an attractive scarlet.

Be sure to start the Borscht a day ahead of time. Not only will it taste better, preparation is easier for the fat can be skimmed from the soup stock when it is cold.

STEP 1: Preceding day, start to make

BORSCHT
1½ pounds plate beef
5 large beets, grated
1 cup grated red cabbage (optional)
2 medium onions, minced
2 medium potatoes, finely cubed
2 teaspoons salt
1½ tablespoons lemon juice
Sour cream

Cover the beef with water, approximately 2 quarts. Add salt. Simmer 1½ to 2 hours. (Or cook in a pressure cooker.) Cool. Meantime, chop or grate vegetables. When meat stock has cooled enough for fat to gather at top, skim off the fat. With a perforated spoon, remove meat. Cut meat into fine pieces for serving. Discard fat and muscle. Then replace meat in stock, along with chopped uncooked vegetables and lemon juice. Add water to make 2½ to 3 quarts. Taste. Add more salt if you think it needs it. Cover. Simmer 1 hour longer. Cool. Place in refrigerator.

This recipe can be easily cut in half for 4, because it's the kind of soup that must be tasted for seasoning anyway, and ingredients may be varied according to what you have in the refrigerator.

The sour cream is added to the soup at serving time.

STEP 2: Also on the preceding day, start preparations for the Piroshki. These are rich pastries filled with meat, fish, vegetables, or cheese. Puff pastry is generally used, but you can use any pastry you like— including regular American pie dough. Sometimes Piroshki are made with yeast dough. We here suggest Cheese Pastry, which must be first chilled for several hours.

CHEESE PASTRY
1 cup flour
¼ teaspoon salt
½ cup (¼ pound) butter or margarine
1 3-ounce package cream cheese

Cut butter and cheese into flour until very fine. Blend thoroughly, using the fingers to work butter and cheese into flour. *Do not add water.* Wrap the dough with waxed paper, place in freezing compartment of refrigerator, and leave there several hours. Then cut dough into small pieces for easier handling, roll out one piece at a time, on a well-floured board, with a well-floured rolling pin, making each about 4 inches square. Place a dab of fish, cabbage, or meat filling (see below) on each square, fold over into a triangle, and press edges together. Bake in a hot oven, 450°F., about 12 minutes, or until golden in color. They will be reheated just before serving.

This same crust is also delicious for making cocktail appetizers, or, filled with jelly, for dessert tarts.

FISH PIROSHKI
¾ cup cooked fish fillet
(flounder, cod, or whitefish)
1 hard-boiled egg
2 tablespoons mayonnaise
Salt, pepper to taste

Chop fish and eggs very fine. Blend with mayonnaise. Add salt and pepper, about ¼ teaspoon salt, ⅛ teaspoon black pepper. Taste. You may want to spice it up with a little dry mustard, about ¼ teaspoon.

CABBAGE PIROSHKI

½ cup shredded cabbage
1 tablespoon fat
¼ teaspoon curry powder
¼ teaspoon salt
1 tablespoon sour cream

Shred cabbage fine, as for cole slaw. Add to melted fat in skillet, along with curry powder and salt. When well blended, remove from fire, add cream. Use about 1 teaspoonful in each square of pastry.

MEAT PIROSHKI

¼ pound ground meat
¼ teaspoon chili powder
¼ teaspoon salt
1 teaspoon grated onion

Blend all ingredients together. Place dab of meat mixture in each square of pastry or dough. (Any ground meat may be used, and it may be either raw or previously cooked.)

STEP 3: Prepare cocktail appetizers. Red caviar with sour cream is appropriate for this Russian meal. Arrange two small bowls on a platter, one containing caviar, the other sour cream, and let people help themselves, spreading their own crackers—or you may spread them to be passed as needed. This is really all you need for an appetizer, but if you want a second thing, celery stuffed with a blend of Roquefort and cream cheese would be good.

STEP 4: Prepare the dessert.

FIG-APRICOT-
RASPBERRY COMPOTE

1 small can whole apricots
1 small can ripe green figs
1 package frozen red raspberries
¼ cup Cointreau

Drain both apricots and figs, saving ½ cup of the sirup from each can. Combine these two fruits and the 1 cup of combined sirup with the Cointreau. Keep chilled in the refrigerator. Remove raspberries from freezing compartment of refrigerator 2 hours before dinner is to be served. Drain part of the juice. Add berries and remaining juice to the other fruit. Keep all in refrigerator until time to serve dessert.

(The above quantity will serve 8. For 4, combine any two of the three fruits suggested, add only 2 tablespoons Cointreau.)

STEP 5: Shortly before guests are due, remove Borscht from refrigerator. If you plan to serve the soup hot, bring to a simmer and let it bubble gently until everyone is ready to go to the table. As you start to reheat the soup, light the oven to reheat the Piroshki.

If the soup is to be served cold, leave in refrigerator until ready to pour into soup plates. (The cold soup is usually strained in advance and served clear.) For either hot or cold soup, be sure there is an ample supply of sour cream. Pass it at the table and let people help themselves.

Dark pumpernickel bread and sweet butter are called for with this meal. Plenty of strong black coffee will be needed to finish it off. Unless you want to copy the Slav custom of tea with lemon, served in glass tumblers.

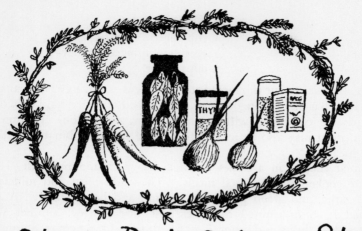

Stews Don't Get in a Stew

MENU

Cocktail Appetizers
Beef Hash with Sherry   Rice
Tomato, Avocado, Water Cress Salad
Meringue Cookies   Fruit Bowl
Coffee

FOR EIGHT

This is a good choice for a buffet supper. The food is already cut up into small pieces, so that guests need not juggle with knife and fork on a precariously tilted plate.

STEP 1: In the morning, prepare

BEEF HASH
WITH SHERRY

4 pounds beef, chuck or round, diced
1 large onion, minced
2 cloves garlic, minced
2 green peppers, minced
1 teaspoon salt
3 large tomatoes, or 1 No. 2½ can

29

2 tablespoons fat
1 cup sherry
1 teaspoon minced parsley
2 cups water

Ask the butcher to cut the meat into 1-inch cubes, then cut it smaller yourself with a sharp knife or a pair of scissors. Leftover beef, lamb, or veal may be combined with fresh meat as an economy measure. Ground meat may also be used, either alone or in combination with cubed meat.

First melt the fat in a skillet or large, heavy aluminum kettle. (A pressure cooker may be used nicely.) Then add meat and minced onion, garlic, and green pepper to the fat, and brown lightly. Add chopped fresh or canned tomatoes, salt, and parsley. Simmer 10 minutes. Add sherry and water. Cover with tight-fitting cover. Simmer 1 hour, or until meat is tender. (If using a pressure cooker, follow directions for beef stew.) Cool. Leave on back of stove, or place in refrigerator, depending on how far away dinnertime remains when you have finished this step.

(This recipe can be cut in half for 4. A little more salt may be needed in proportion. Taste to make sure.)

STEP 2: Prepare the dessert. A very easy and impressive dessert for a buffet is

MERINGUE COOKIES

Make refrigerator cookies, using a standard recipe or a prepared cookie mix. When thoroughly chilled, slice thin, bake according to directions. Next top each cookie with a scant half teaspoon jelly or jam, and spread stiffly beaten, sweetened egg white over the top. One egg white with 1 tablespoon confectioners' sugar will make enough meringue for a dozen cookies. Place cookies in oven reduced to 325°F. for 8 to 10 minutes.

STEP 3: Prepare cocktail appetizers. You might offer toasted coconut chips, Cheetos, and

CURRIED SARDINE CANAPÉS
1 can sardines
1 3-ounce package cream cheese
Few drops lemon juice
¼ teaspoon curry powder
1 teaspoon sweet or sour cream

Mash sardines with a fork, first removing backbone and ugly bits of skin. Keep light and fluffy. In a separate bowl, whip cream cheese, adding a little sour cream or heavy sweet cream to soften. Season with curry powder. Add lemon juice to taste, adding more if the first few drops don't seem to be enough. Go easy on the lemon at first, though. You could easily add too much. Serve in a bowl surrounded by potato chips and let people dunk, or serve with a butter spreader.

STEP 4: Wash 1½ cups rice through several waters, until water is clear. You will remove more starch (and the grains will be drier and more separate) if you stir the rice around briskly in a kettle instead of simply holding it under the faucet in a strainer. When rice is well cleaned, place in heavy kettle, one with a tight-fitting cover, add 4 cups water, ½ teaspoon salt. (Or follow directions on rice package.) Cover. Do not cook until 20 minutes before dinner is to be served.

STEP 5: Clean water cress. Place in bowl which has been rubbed with garlic. Chill tomato and avocado, but do not cut up until a short time before guests are due. Keep all salad ingredients in refrigerator. Mix French dressing, adding a pinch of curry powder.

STEP 6: Set table. Put coffee and water in pot. Arrange cookies in a serving bowl. Then have a nice, long bath and get yourself completely relaxed.

STEP 7: Make a paste of 2 tablespoons flour with a little water added slowly until it's the consistency of thin cream. Add this to hash. Reheat hash slowly. Have hash at a simmering temperature when guests are due. If a long wait appears possible, turn off the heat under the stew, and bring back to a simmer when everyone is ready to eat.

STEP 8: About the time the guests are enjoying a second round of cocktails, turn the heat on under the rice. Watch until it comes to a boil, then turn heat as low as possible. Consult your watch, and let the rice cook exactly 20 minutes. It should have absorbed all the liquid, leaving little "gopher holes" here and there.

Meantime, arrange salad for table. Reheat hash. By time rice is cooked, everything else should be ready, including your guests.

32

MENU

Cocktail Appetizers
Ragout of Veal with Mushrooms
Noodles   Broccoli
Tomato and Romaine Salad
Peaches with White Wine Sauce   Coffee

FOR SIX

STEP 1: In the morning (or on the preceding day), prepare

RAGOUT OF VEAL	2½ pounds veal, cubed
WITH MUSHROOMS	½ cup minced onion
	½ pound mushrooms
	4 tablespoons butter
	½ teaspoon salt
	1 cup water
	½ cup sour cream

Melt 3 tablespoons butter in a heavy skillet or kettle, one which has a tight-fitting cover. Brown the cubed meat. Remove. Add the chopped onion. Brown lightly. Then add the meat once again. Add salt and water. Cover. Simmer 1 hour, or until tender. Meantime, clean mushrooms, but do not peel. If they are small, use the whole caps. If large, cube both caps and stems. Place in separate saucepan with remaining 1 tablespoon butter. When butter has melted, add ½ cup water and ¼ teaspoon salt. Cover. Parboil 4 or 5 minutes, saving liquor. When ragout is tender, add mushrooms and their liquor. Do not continue cooking after mushrooms are added, or distinctive mushroom flavor will be lost.

(Canned mushrooms may be used when the fresh are not in season. Use the liquor in the can.)

Keep ragout on back of stove or in refrigerator until serving time. Sour cream is to be added last.

STEP 2: Prepare cocktail appetizers. Chive cheese, to be spread on potato chips, crisp bacon rind (the commercial kind), and a shrimp-avocado spread for canapés would go well with this meal.

SHRIMP-AVOCADO
CANAPÉS

1 small can (3 ounce) shrimp
1 avocado, very soft
½ cup mayonnaise
1 teaspoon capers
1 tablespoon catsup
¼ teaspoon salt
Dash black pepper
½ teaspoon dry mustard
1 teaspoon curry powder
Few drops lemon juice

Mash avocado to pulp. Drain shrimp, crumble to small pieces. Blend avocado and shrimp with mayonnaise, capers, catsup, salt, pepper, mustard, and curry powder. Add the lemon juice last. As a matter of caution, add only ½ teaspoon curry powder at first, and taste. Some curry powders are much sharper than others, and a whole teaspoonful might be too much for your taste. Keep in refrigerator until guests arrive. Then serve the bowl of spread on a platter surrounded with crackers and let guests help themselves.

STEP 3: Clean broccoli. Cut up into small pieces. The smaller the pieces, the more quickly can broccoli be cooked, and the more quickly it is cooked, the better the flavor. Five minutes is often enough if the broccoli is fresh. For broccoli that is beginning to yellow slightly, add a tiny pinch of baking soda to the cooking water. This hastens the cooking process and keeps the vegetables a bright green. Don't do it unless the broccoli seems old, however, for the soda does snuff out some of the vitamins. Cold water may be added to the cut-up vegetable as much as an hour before it is to be cooked. Then all you have to do later is turn the heat on under the saucepan.

STEP 4: Clean salad greens and cut into serving pieces. Place in bowl in which garlic has been mashed to a pulp. Prepare French dressing. Clean tomatoes but do not cut up until serving time.

STEP 5: Prepare dessert. First, the

WHITE WINE SAUCE   ½ cup sugar
                          ½ tablespoon cornstarch
                          Grated rind 1 lemon
                          Juice ½ lemon
                          2 egg yolks
                          1 cup white wine
                          ⅛ teaspoon salt
                          2 egg whites

Mix sugar and cornstarch. Add lemon rind and juice. Beat yolks until thick, add to cornstarch mixture along with wine and salt. Place saucepan on range, stirring constantly over medium heat until boiling point is reached (sauce will begin to plop). Remove from the heat and stir in the egg whites, which have been beaten until so stiff that the bowl can be turned upside down. Keep the sauce in the refrigerator until ready to serve.

This sauce may be made with any white wine, dry or sweet. It is excellent with sherry. It will keep for some time in the refrigerator and is good with any fresh fruit, or on cake slices.

STEP 6: If fresh peaches are to be used, peel them during the last hour before guests are expected, cut into slices, then cover with sugar and a little lemon juice or white wine to prevent turning brown. If using frozen peaches, take from freezing compartment to thaw several hours before dinner, leave on lower refrigerator shelf. Do not remove from package until shortly before guests are due. Then mix thoroughly with wine sauce and pile in dessert dishes. Keep dishes in refrigerator until dessert time.

STEP 7: Set table. Put coffee and water in pot. Get yourself ready. Take a last look around to be sure everything is in order.

STEP 8: Half fill a large kettle with water. Add 1 teaspoon salt. Open noodles, have right amount ready to plunge into boiling water when time comes. Prepare a paste to thicken ragout, using 2 tablespoons flour, or 1 tablespoon cornstarch, adding water until the consistency of cream. Add this to ragout. Then heat ragout to simmering and keep at simmer until guests begin to arrive.

While you are mixing drinks, start the water for the noodles. After the water is boiling briskly, add noodles and cook 12 to 14 minutes. Drain. Add 1 tablespoon butter. Now add sour cream to the ragout and reheat to simmering. Turn the heat on under the broccoli, cook until barely tender when pricked with a fork, then drain, add butter and a few drops of lemon juice.

These last-minute steps can be taken care of after everyone has arrived. In fact, wait until conversation is sparkling, your guests busily talking to one another, then disappear into the kitchen. Everyone will admire your aplomb.

MENU

Cocktail Appetizers
Lamb Stew à la Grecque
Rice   Green Salad
French Bread
Yogurt with Blackberry Jam   Coffee

FOR SIX

STEP 1: In the morning, or on the preceding day, prepare

LAMB STEW À LA GRECQUE   3 lamb shanks
3 tablespoons oil or fat
3 or 4 cloves garlic, minced
2 medium onions, sliced
1 No. 2½ can tomatoes
¾ teaspoon salt
½ teaspoon oregano
½ teaspoon thyme
1 tablespoon cornstarch
½ cup water

When you order lamb shanks, ask the butcher to crack the bone in several places. Cut through the meat so that you have the right size for serving. Heat the olive oil (or vegetable fat) in a heavy skillet or kettle. Brown the lamb in this. Add the garlic and onion. Brown slightly. Add tomatoes, salt, and herbs. Cover. Bring to a boil, turn the heat low, and simmer 2 hours, or until so tender meat is ready to come from the bone. (Or it can be cooked in a pressure cooker, following the directions for lamb stew.) When meat is cooked, cool, put aside until shortly before serving time. The thickening, a paste of cornstarch and water, will be added then.

STEP 2: For the YOGURT WITH BLACKBERRY JAM, order 3 half pints of yogurt to serve 6. Mix ¾ cup sugar with this quantity of yogurt, or 2 tablespoons of sugar to each individual serving. Chill. *Just before serving*, spoon chilled, sweetened yogurt into dessert dishes, add two tablespoons blackberry jam to each dish, letting the jam sink in.

STEP 3: Prepare cocktail appetizers. In honor of the Greek stew, you might serve the moon-shaped Greek black olives which are put up in red wine vinegar. These are imported, usually found only in Greek groceries, but they are worth a search, for they are the tastiest black olives of all to serve as appetizers. You might also have pistachio nuts and

SALMON CAPER	1 3-ounce can salmon
CANAPÉS	1 tablespoon capers
	Mayonnaise
	Few drops lemon juice

Break up the salmon lightly with a fork. Remove bone and skin. Drain excess oil. Add capers. Blend in just enough mayonnaise to bind into a spread. Sprinkle with lemon juice. Arrange in a bowl, to be spread on crackers or melba toast squares.

STEP 4: Wash rice through several waters, stirring briskly to get rid of excess starch. Place in saucepan, adding water and salt in correct measure. Cover saucepan. Leave on back of stove until 20 minutes before meal is to be served.

STEP 5: Clean salad. Cut into serving pieces. Place in bowl which has been rubbed with garlic, keep in refrigerator until ready to serve. Mix French dressing.

STEP 6: Set table. Put coffee and water in pot. Get dressed. Relax.

STEP 7: Add thickening to lamb stew, making a cornstarch paste the consistency of thin cream. Reheat to simmering about time guests are due, adding more water if necessary. (A certain amount of liquid evaporates as the stew stands, so more water is usually necessary.) Twenty minutes before serving time, cook rice, mix salad, then call guests to the table as soon as the rice is ready.

MENU

Cocktail Appetizers
Beef à la Stroganoff
Rice   Frenched Green Beans
Lettuce, Radish, Cucumber Salad
Cherry Heering Sundae   Coffee

FOR EIGHT

Another good choice for a buffet supper. Easy to eat without a knife. Easy to serve. Everybody will like it.

STEP 1: Prepare

BEEF À LA STROGANOFF

3½ pounds beef, chuck or round
3 medium onions, minced
2 tablespoons tomato catsup
1 cup water
1 cup sour cream
1 tablespoon cornstarch
¾ teaspoon salt

Use scissors to cut the beef into small pieces, the size of your fingernail. Place beef, onions, catsup, salt, and water in a kettle or pressure cooker. Bring to a boil, simmer 1 hour, or until tender. (In a pressure cooker, allow 10 minutes' cooking time after steam is at correct pressure.) Cool. Do not add thickening or sour cream until shortly before serving time.

This can be made a day or two ahead of time. It will improve with waiting.

(To serve 4, you can simply reduce the above ingredients by half. Taste for salt, use liquid enough to make sauce the consistency of thin cream.)

STEP 2: Slice beans lengthwise. Wrap in waxed paper or place in plastic bag, store in refrigerator. Beans can be placed in saucepan with water and salt an hour before dinnertime, so that you only need to turn the heat on under them to cook.

STEP 3: Prepare cocktail appetizers. You might have potato chips, salted pumpkin seeds, and

LOBSTER SALAD	1 lobster tail
CANAPÉS	½ cup mayonnaise
	¾ tablespoon catsup
	2 sweet gherkins, minced
	½ teaspoon capers
	Few drops lemon juice
	¼ teaspoon salt

Parboil the lobster tail 10 minutes, or until pink. Remove shell when cool. Slice very thin, then cut into smaller pieces. Mix with remaining ingredients. Taste. You may want more salt or lemon juice. To serve, place in a bowl set in the middle of a platter. Surround with crackers. Let people spread their own canapés.

STEP 4: Wash rice through several waters, stirring briskly to get rid of excess starch. Add 4 cups water, ½ teaspoon salt to 1½ cups rice (or follow directions on package). Keep in saucepan on back of stove until serving time, then allow exactly 20 minutes to cook.

STEP 5: Wash and cut up lettuce, radishes, and cucumbers. Add to bowl which has previously been rubbed with garlic. Keep in refrigerator until serving time.

STEP 6: The dessert, CHERRY HEERING SUNDAE, cannot be arranged until the last minute. Until then, keep the ice cream in the freezing compartment of your refrigerator. Meantime, get out dessert dishes, and beside them have a bottle of Cherry Heering liqueur. Use this as a dessert sauce over the ice cream. Other thick, sweet liqueurs may be used in the same way, but this one with its red color is particularly attractive.

STEP 7: Set the table. Put coffee and water in pot. Get dressed. Relax.

STEP 8: Add thickening to Stroganoff. Reheat to simmering. After guests have all arrived, turn the heat on under the rice, add salt and water to the string beans, boil until barely tender when pricked with a fork. Add sour cream to Stroganoff. When the rice is cooked, both the string beans and Stroganoff should also be ready to serve. Toss dressing into salad. Set out the food on the buffet and urge people to start helping themselves.

MENU

Cocktail Appetizers
Pungent Pot Roast
Noodles   Green Salad
Brandied Peaches on Cake   Coffee

FOR EIGHT

One of the nicest things about this pot roast is the fragrance it gives off while cooking. Everyone will think you're making up a batch of homemade chili sauce.

STEP 1: Prepare the pot roast for cooking, but do not actually start cooking it until 2 hours before guests are due. Meantime, it will be getting tender from the spices and vinegar you add as a marinade.

PUNGENT POT ROAST

3½ pounds boneless pot roast
1 teaspoon meat tenderizer
1 teaspoon cinnamon
½ teaspoon ground cloves
1 or 2 garlic cloves, minced
½ medium onion, sliced
1 green pepper, minced
4 tomatoes, peeled and cubed
    (or 2 No. 303 cans tomatoes)
3 tablespoons vinegar
2 tablespoons cornstarch

Mix spices, meat tenderizer, vinegar, onion, green pepper, and garlic. Spread this mixture over the top of the meat. (Salt should not be necessary because of the meat tenderizer, but since there are several meat tenderizers on the market and the ingredients vary, you had better taste the sauce critically, after the meat has been cooking an hour or more, to see if it has enough salt.) Let the meat marinate for 2 hours or more.

Late in the afternoon, 2 hours before guests are due, add the cut-up tomatoes, or the canned tomatoes, and start cooking the meat. Keep it simmering until you are ready to serve dinner. *Just before serving dinner,* remove the meat from the sauce, and make a paste of cornstarch with a little water, then add this to the sauce for thickening, letting the sauce simmer for 5 minutes.

STEP 2: Prepare the dessert. For BRANDIED PEACHES ON CAKE, bake a plain white cake in a square or oblong cake pan, using a prepared mix or any standard recipe. While cake is in the oven, open a can of "home style" peaches, slice or cut up peaches, and add a cupful of the canned sirup along with 2 tablespoons of brandy or liqueur. Chill the peaches in this flavored sirup *until dessert time.* You will meantime have cut the cake into serving pieces, arranged on dessert plates. To serve, spoon the brandy sirup over the cake, letting it soak in, top with cut-up peaches, and garnish with whipped cream or prepared topping.

STEP 3: Prepare cocktail appetizers. Besides one or two crunchy things, like popcorn or pretzels, you might have

CURRIED EGG	1 hard-cooked egg, chopped fine
CANAPÉS	¼ teaspoon curry powder
	Mayonnaise to bind
	¼ teaspoon salt

The egg should be minced as fine as hominy grits. Add curry powder and salt and enough mayonnaise to make a smooth paste. For color, if you wish, you may add very finely chopped black olives and/or red pimiento. Place in a bowl, keep chilled in the refrigerator until guests are due, then place in the center of a platter surrounded with crackers.

STEP 4: Wash, cut up salad greens, into serving pieces. Place in plastic bag, keep in refrigerator. Within the last hour before dinner, place salad greens in a bowl well rubbed with garlic, keeping this bowl in the refrigerator until the salad course is due.

STEP 5: Set out noodles on the stove, beside a large kettle half filled with water to which 1 teaspoon of salt has been added. Start heating water when you mix the first cocktails.

STEP 6: Set table. Put coffee and water in pot. Get dressed.

STEP 7: After guests have arrived and the first drinks have been served, cook the noodles in rapidly boiling water for 12 to 14 minutes, add thickening to pot roast sauce, put salad together. Between courses, add peaches and whipped cream to cake, and start the coffee as you add the finishing touches to the dessert.

MENU

Cocktail Appetizers
Roast Beef Stew   Potatoes
Salad of Romaine, Olives, Avocado
Raspberry Flummery   Coffee

FOR EIGHT

This is a good second-day dinner when you have house guests. The first night you produce a beautiful rib roast. Naturally there are some good slices left for cold cuts. But there are also hunks of meat that do not slice easily. These make the basis of a stew.

STEP 1: Look over the leftover roast carefully. If a considerable amount is left intact, slice off the sliceable sections and wrap in aluminum foil. Put these in the refrigerator for cold cuts or sandwiches. Now place the bones and the rest of the meat in a kettle. Add 2 or 3 cups of water and ½ teaspoon salt. Cover. Simmer 1 hour. Cool. Remove the bones, cut off all the meat and put the meat aside. Add to the stock the following:

> 1 dozen small white onions
> 2 carrots, diced
> 1 teaspoon minced parsley
> 1 bay leaf
> 1 bouillon cube
> ¼ pound mushrooms, diced
> 2 tablespoons tomato catsup
> ½ cup white wine

You may add potatoes, or boil them separately, as you prefer. The flavor of the potatoes is better if they are cooked separately just before serving. (If you are short on meat for this stew, add more vegetables.

Frozen lima beans are good. They can be added during the last 5 minutes of cooking.) Simmer the vegetables 20 minutes, or until tender. Then add leftover gravy and all the bits of meat. Taste for seasoning. More salt may be necessary. Cool. Keep in refrigerator until dinnertime.

STEP 2: Prepare the dessert.

RASPBERRY FLUMMERY	2 packages frozen raspberries
	White wine (about ½ cup)
	5 tablespoons cornstarch
	½ cup water
	½ cup sugar

Thaw berries completely. Carefully drain juice. Measure. Add white wine enough to make 2 cups. Dissolve cornstarch in cold water. Add sugar. Combine with juice-wine mixture and bring to a boil, then turn heat low and simmer 3 or 4 minutes, stirring almost continuously. Add berries gently, simmer another 1 minute without stirring. Pour into molds. Chill. Unmold to serve. Garnish with whipped cream or prepared topping.

To serve 4, use 1 package of berries, 2½ tablespoons of cornstarch, 4 tablespoons water, 4 tablespoons sugar.

This can be made of the juice alone, a fine way to use raspberry juice when the berries are being used in some other way, as in tarts, for instance. To 1 pint of juice, use 3 tablespoons of cornstarch, simmer for a full 5 minutes.

(BLUEBERRY FLUMMERY can be made in the same way with canned blueberries, or the juice alone used if the berries are needed for another dessert. The pudding will keep in the refrigerator for days.)

STEP 3: Prepare cocktail appetizers. If this meal is for "home folks," keep the appetizers simple. Chive cheese to spread on potato chips, olives, carrot sticks. If you want to be a bit different, have

MARINATED CARROT	2 tablespoons vinegar
STICKS	2 tablespoons oil
	1 garlic clove
	½ teaspoon savory salt
	¼ teaspoon salt

Cut carrots into thin, short sticks. Lay in the marinade so that the carrots are at least partially covered. Drain to serve.

STEP 4: Wash and cut up salad greens, place in bowl rubbed with garlic, keep in refrigerator until time to serve.

STEP 5: Make French dressing with lemon instead of vinegar, add a bit of crumbled blue cheese. Chill avocados, but do not peel until the last hour before dinner. Keep black olives (those processed in brine are best) and avocados side by side so that all salad ingredients will be at hand when you need them.

STEP 6: Relax until your guests show signs of being ready for dinner. Then get out the cocktail appetizers, and while they enjoy this first course in the living room, put the potatoes on to boil. Get the stew from the refrigerator. Add thickening of 2 tablespoons of flour or one of cornstarch thinned with water to a smooth paste. Reheat the stew. While stew simmers, peel the avocados and put the salad together. Now you are ready.

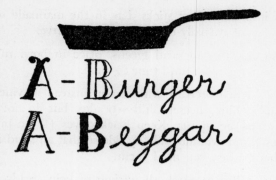

A-Burger A-Beggar

MENU

Cocktail Appetizers
Steak Tartare
Tomatoes with Roquefort Dressing
Green Salad   Assorted Breads
Camembert Cheese   Coffee

FOR TEN

This is a wonderful guest menu for a hot summer evening. Nothing has to be cooked except the coffee. "Steak Tartare" is also sometimes called "Beefsteak Américain" abroad—even though it is known to relatively few Americans. Another name for it is "Cannibal Steak."

STEP 1: From the butcher, order top round or sirloin ground very fine, put through the chopper at least twice—better, three times. Since the meat is to be served raw, have it delivered no earlier than noon of the day it is to be served. You may, if you wish, mix the "steak" at table. In this case, simply have all the ingredients ready and well chilled.

STEAK TARTARE	
	4 pounds top round or sirloin, ground very fine
	2 raw eggs
	3 teaspoons salt (1 tablespoon)
	2 tablespoons grated onion and juice
	2 tablespoons capers

44

The eggs are to be beaten until light and frothy, at the last minute before dinner is to be served. Whether or not the "steak" is mixed at table, it should be put together only a short time before it is to be eaten. Otherwise, the meat turns dark in color and looks less appetizing.

For 6 persons, use 3 pounds meat, 1 egg, 2 teaspoons salt, 1 tablespoon each onion juice and capers.

STEP 2: The cocktail appetizers should all be light and crunchy for this warm evening. Stuffed celery, radishes, olives. Potato chips may be put out to accompany both cocktails and the "Steak Tartare." You may use two different spreads to stuff the celery. Garlic cheese for one, for the other, perhaps

TUNA FISH PÂTÉ

1 7-ounce can tuna fish
1 tablespoon soy sauce
1 tablespoon catsup
½ teaspoon salt
1 scallion, minced fine
2 tablespoons mayonnaise
⅛ teaspoon cayenne pepper

Rub bowl with crushed garlic. Remove shreds. Add tuna fish, flake very fine with a fork. With the addition of each ingredient, mash down until you have a very smooth paste. Chill thoroughly.

STEP 3: Wash salad greens. Cut into serving pieces. Store in refrigerator.

STEP 4: Prepare Roquefort dressing for tomatoes (crumbled Roquefort cheese in French dressing), plain French dressing for the tossed salad. Slice tomatoes, marinate in the Roquefort dressing in the refrigerator.

STEP 5: Set the table. In the living room, have cocktail appetizers set out. In the dining room, put cheese on a platter, bread in bowls or on platters, etc. Put water and coffee in pot. Then get yourself set, and relax.

STEP 6: Greet your guests. When everyone seems ready, start taking things out of the refrigerator. All you have to do at the last minute is beat the eggs, then mix up the "steak."

Inevitably, some people are squeamish about eating raw meat. For that reason, better serve this meal to people you know to be open-minded about food.

MENU

Cauliflower with Curry Sauce
Burgers with Barbecue Sauce
Buns
Potato Chips   Corn on Cob
Fruit Bowl   Coffee

FOR TEN

This is a good menu for an outdoor barbecue. You'll notice that silverware is unnecessary. Plates can be of paper, then tossed in the fire afterward to eliminate dishwashing.

STEP 1: In the morning, or on the preceding day, prepare

BARBECUE SAUCE

¼ cup tomato catsup
1 teaspoon horse-radish
½ teaspoon chili powder
½ teaspoon dry mustard
2 tablespoons vinegar
4 tablespoons oil
½ teaspoon salt
2 cloves garlic

Mash garlic in bowl, until nothing but shreds remain. Throw these away. Add remaining ingredients. Place bowl in cool place, but not in refrigerator, because oil may thicken. (If prepared the day before, keep in refrigerator overnight, but remove several hours before dinner is to be served.)

There are two ways to prepare the burgers. One is to grill them over the open fire, with the meat resting on the grill itself. The juices are lost in this way, but the meat captures some of the charcoal flavor. If you cook the burgers this way, marinate the flattened cakes in the sauce before cooking, and have some of the sauce in a bowl beside the grill for people to spoon over their burgers after they have put them in buns.

The other method is to cook the burgers in a skillet, spooning the Barbecue Sauce over them after they have been browned on both sides. This captures the essence from the meat, which is blended with the sauce. Each method has its merits. Do whichever appeals most to you.

STEP 2: Separate cauliflower into small flowerlets. These are to be eaten raw, dunked in the sauce.

CURRY SAUCE	1 cup mayonnaise
FOR CAULIFLOWER	1 teaspoon lemon juice
	1 teaspoon curry powder
	¼ teaspoon salt

Blend ingredients well. Keep in refrigerator until serving time. Then place sauce in a small bowl which will fit in center of platter with chilled cauliflower pieces around it.

STEP 3: Wash fruit and chill. Select fruits that can be eaten with the fingers, such as grapes, bananas, nectarines, apples, or pears.

STEP 4: Strip silk from ears of corn. Wrap the corn in aluminum foil, first spreading with softened butter, then dust with salt. Corn wrapped in this way can be roasted in the coals of the barbecue pit.

STEP 5: Pat hamburger into flat cakes. Add ¾ teaspoon salt to each pound of ground meat. Better allow 2 hamburgers to each person, 6 hamburgers to the pound. Order the same number of buns. Marinate burgers in barbecue sauce if to be grilled right over fire (see above).

STEP 6: Have potato chips, buns, and all the other foods ready to carry to out-of-doors picnic table. Get dressed. Relax until first guests arrive.

48

MENU

Cocktail Appetizers
Hamburgers Hollandaise
Broccoli   Baked or Au Gratin Potatoes
Celery, Olives
Rhubarb Pie   Coffee

FOR SIX

STEP 1: In the morning, prepare

HOLLANDAISE SAUCE

½ cup butter (¼ pound)
2 or 3 egg yolks
⅓ cup boiling water
¼ teaspoon salt
1 teaspoon lemon juice

Divide the butter into 3 parts. Place the first part in the top of a double boiler with 2 egg yolks and 1 teaspoon of lemon juice. Have hot water in the bottom of the double boiler but take care that the water is not deep enough to touch the top part of the boiler, and do not let the water come to a boil. The safest way is to turn the heat off altogether after the water underneath is hot. Stir the butter, egg, and lemon mixture until the butter is melted. Add the second part of butter, continue to stir, then the third part. When the mixture is thick, add the boiling water a tablespoonful at a time, continuing to stir all the time, until thick and creamy. Season with salt at the very end. Place the Hollandaise in the refrigerator and leave there until serving time.

If the sauce curdles, drop the third egg yolk in another bowl and add the curdled sauce to it gradually, stirring all the while. This is a trick that never fails.

STEP 2: Well in advance, make

RHUBARB PIE

Pastry for a 9-inch pie
4 cups diced uncooked rhubarb
6 tablespoons flour
1½ cups sugar
1 tablespoon butter

Roll out pastry, using your favorite pie crust recipe or a prepared mix.

Spread 3 tablespoons flour over the bottom crust, then part of the sugar. Pile up the diced rhubarb evenly over the dough. Sift sugar and flour, mixed together, over rhubarb. Dot butter over the fruit. Add the top crust. Flute edges and prick top crust with a fork. Bake in a hot oven, 400°F., for 40 minutes, or until crust is golden brown.

STEP 3: For a very delicious and unusual appetizer, prepare

RADISH BUTTER   1 bunch radishes, grated
                                 ¼ pound butter

Either grate the radishes, or put through a food chopper. You should have 4 tablespoons or ¼ cup grated radish. Blend with butter which has been softened to a creamy consistency. Keep soft until ready to serve, for while the combination is delicious as long as the butter is soft, it changes altogether if the butter gets hard. The butter can be left at room temperature for 4 or 5 hours without any harm being done. Serve on melba toast rounds.

Along with the Radish Butter, you might serve olives, Cheetos, and Curried Tuna Fish Canapés.

STEP 4: Cut broccoli into small pieces. An hour before dinner, the broccoli may be placed in a saucepan, salt and cold water added to it, so that nothing remains to be done but turn on the heat under it 10 minutes before the meal is to be served.

STEP 5: For the HAMBURGERS HOLLANDAISE, cut bread into rounds a little larger than the flattened burger cakes. These are to be lightly toasted.

The meat cakes should be large, allowing 4 to the pound. Use ¾ teaspoon salt to each pound of meat. Arrange meat and bread rounds on broiler pan, but do not put into oven until 10 minutes before dinner is to be served. Oven should be preheated to 500°F.

STEP 6: Scrub celery, cut into serving pieces, arrange with olives in relish dish. Keep in refrigerator until time to serve.

STEP 7: If you are having baked potatoes, allow 1 to each person. Scrub thoroughly before placing in the oven. Baked potatoes are by far the easiest, but they do not wait well. Large potatoes require a good hour for baking, so if your guests are the kind that might be hours late, either select smallish potatoes and bake them at high heat, 500°F., for 40 minutes, after the first guests have arrived, or prepare

POTATOES AU GRATIN

6 medium potatoes
2 tablespoons butter
2 tablespoons flour
2 cups milk
½ cup grated sharp cheese
½ teaspoon salt

Parboil potatoes. Peel and dice. Make a cream sauce of the butter, flour, and milk. When smooth, add salt and cheese. Mix with potatoes. Pour into greased casserole. Place in oven. Bake 1 hour at 350°F. This means turning on the oven 20 to 30 minutes before guests are due.

STEP 8: Set table. Put coffee and water in pot. Get dressed. Relax.

STEP 9: After guests have arrived and first round of cocktails has been served, turn up oven to 500°F. for broiling. When oven has reached this heat (allow 5 minutes) place bread on broiler and toast lightly. Remove to a platter. Broil the hamburgers until well browned on each side.

Start the broccoli cooking as the burgers grill. Get Hollandaise from the refrigerator and place the bowl containing it over a kettle or saucepan which has about an inch of very hot but not boiling water in the bottom. Cover saucepan with a towel. Only 2 or 3 minutes are required to soften the sauce. As burgers are removed from the broiling oven, place them on the toast rounds, and pour sauce over the meat. These must be served at once.

MENU

Cocktail Appetizers
Magnificent Meat Balls
Peas   Baked or Au Gratin Potatoes
Lettuce and Cucumber Salad
Jelly Tarts   Coffee

FOR SIX

This is a good choice for an evening when you're having neighbors or old friends in for supper. It's not pretentious, but it is different enough from ordinary meat balls to make it company fare.

STEP 1: Prepare the dessert. Either the preceding day, or early in the morning, make Cheese Pastry, leaving in the freezing compartment of the refrigerator several hours to chill thoroughly. To roll out, cut the dough into 6 portions and form squares. Place a tablespoon of currant, guava, or quince jelly in the center of each. Fold over into a triangle, press the edges together with the tines of a fork. Bake in a very hot oven, 450°F., for 10 to 15 minutes, or until golden brown.

STEP 2: Prepare the meat balls for baking, leaving in a suitable baking dish, in the oven, until shortly before guests are due.

MAGNIFICENT MEAT BALLS	
	2 pounds ground beef
	2 cups canned tomatoes
	1 cup fine bread crumbs
	1 egg
	1¼ teaspoons salt
	1 teaspoon grated onion and juice
	12 slices bacon
	½ cup sour cream

"Hamburger beef" will do for this dish, though ground chuck is better. Mix together the beef, 1 cup of the tomatoes, bread crumbs, egg, salt, and onion juice. Form into good-sized balls. Wrap each with a slice of bacon, overlapping the bacon carefully and placing this overlap bottom side down. Place in a large flat baking dish so that bacon strips make a crisscross pattern. The sour cream and the remaining cup of tomatoes will be added later. Put baking dish in oven, but do not turn on oven until 15 minutes before guests are due.

STEP 3: Prepare cocktail appetizers. A good selection would be a smoked swordfish spread and garlic olives. If you use swordfish, break up with a fork, and mix with either softened butter or cream cheese to make a paste. Canned tuna fish may be prepared in the same way. This is the way you make

GARLIC OLIVES

Add to a bottle of large whole green olives a peeled whole clove of garlic, ½ teaspoon savory salt, and a tablespoon of red wine vinegar, or of cider vinegar mixed with dry red wine. (Or you can add the cider vinegar alone.) Let olives marinate in this for several hours. Garlic flavor will be absorbed.

STEP 4: Cut up lettuce into serving pieces. Wash and rewash, then drain carefully. Place in plastic bag or in vegetable freshener until serving time. Slice unpeeled cucumber paper-thin. Wrap in waxed paper.

STEP 5: If you are having baked potatoes, scrub each well and place in oven. However, if you decide on Au Gratin Potatoes (see advice in preceding menu), parboil potatoes, arrange in cheese cream sauce in baking dish. Turn on oven 20 minutes before guests are expected for a total of 1 hour's baking time.

STEP 6: Shell peas. Place in saucepan along with 2 or 3 pods to help keep the peas green. Do not add water until time to cook. (Or serve frozen peas, adding boiling water to the peas about 5 minutes before dinner is to be served.)

STEP 7: Set table. Put coffee and water in pot. Get dressed. Relax.

STEP 8: Turn on the oven to 350°F. 15 to 20 minutes before you expect the first guests to arrive. This allows 40 minutes' baking time for the meat balls after people arrive, enough for a couple of rounds of cocktails. Start the peas cooking only after everyone has arrived. Remember the secret of full-flavored vegetables is to use the smallest possible amount of cooking water, cook the shortest possible time, and serve as soon after cooking as possible.

Mix salad in bowl rubbed with garlic, add condiments, vinegar, oil. Now look into the oven. The bacon around the meat balls should be crisp. Take out the dish, pour off the excess bacon fat by holding a platter or large lid over the baking dish while you tilt it. Another way is to dip out the excess fat with a large spoon. Blend sour cream and tomato together, then pour over the meat balls in dish and return to oven. Turn off heat.

By the time the peas are cooked, the meat balls will be ready to serve, and everything else should be under control.

The beauty of a sauce such as this for the meat balls is that it saves the meat from drying out if, in spite of everything, dinner must be postponed for hours. Even if the meat cools in the dish, it can be reheated quickly without loss of flavor or texture.

MENU

Cocktail Appetizers
Chili Corn Pie
Tomato, Lima Bean, Avocado Salad
Hot Rolls
Strawberries with Yogurt   Coffee

FOR SIX

Here's a good emergency meal. The chili may come out of a can. To extend and enrich the single can, add more ground meat and additional chili powder. The corn meal crust can be made with corn muffin mix. The rolls may be the brown 'n' serve kind. Strawberries may be frozen.

STEP 1: For the CHILI CORN PIE, pour a can of chili con carne into a casserole dish. Add 1 pound hamburger, ½ teaspoon chili powder, stirring to mix thoroughly. (Or you could, if it's easier, use 2 cans of chili.) Next, add egg and milk to a package of corn muffin mix. Spread this over the top of the chili. After the guests have arrived, you will place the casserole in an oven preheated to 400°F. and bake 25 minutes, or until corn meal crust is golden brown.

STEP 2: For the dessert, STRAWBERRIES WITH YOGURT, if using frozen strawberries, take package from freezing compartment 2 hours before mealtime. It may be thawed on a lower shelf of refrigerator. One package will be plenty. If you prefer fresh strawberries, slice and

54

sugar them hours in advance and chill in the refrigerator, or prepare them for serving half an hour before dinner, whichever suits best. One pint fresh berries will be enough.

Three half pints of yogurt will be needed for 6 people. Mix 2 tablespoons of sugar with each serving of yogurt, or ¾ cup of sugar with the 3 half pints. Divide into serving dishes. Just before serving, top each dish of yogurt with strawberries.

STEP 3: Prepare vegetables for salad, but do not cut up either tomatoes or avocados until serving time. Break off one half package of frozen baby limas, return rest of limas, still frozen, to freezing compartment. Boil the limas in the usual way. Drain. Keep in a bowl until ready to mix with other ingredients, or marinate in French dressing. Cut up romaine, or lettuce, into serving pieces. Wash thoroughly. Keep in plastic bag, or in salad bowl already rubbed with garlic. Mix all vegetables with dressing at the table.

STEP 4: Arrange cocktail appetizers in bowls. A selection of ready-to-serve appetizers from the grocery will be easiest: perhaps the pink, shrimp-flavored curls, pretzels, and nuts.

STEP 5: Place the casserole in the oven. Twenty minutes later shove the "brown 'n' serve" rolls in the oven. Preparation time is a matter of minutes.

Here's another variation of the same idea:

CHILI WITH AVOCADOS

Heat 1 or 2 cans of chili, enriching with additional chopped beef if desired. Serve on a bed of steamed rice. Spread slices of avocados fanwise over the top.

If you are really in a hurry, use precooked rice, and you'll have dinner ready in about 10 minutes.

MENU

Cocktail Appetizers
Meat Balls in Pickle Sauce
Rice   Tomato Salad
Apricot Delight   Coffee

FOR SIX

STEP 1: Prepare

MEAT BALLS IN PICKLE SAUCE	1½ pounds ground beef 1 egg 1 teaspoon salt 1 cup bread crumbs ½ cup milk 2 tablespoons bacon fat
SAUCE	½ pound mushrooms 3 cups water ½ teaspoon salt 2 cloves garlic, minced ½ cup minced onion ½ cup catsup 2 tablespoons minced parsley 2 tablespoons Worcestershire sauce 1 tablespoon cornstarch

Soak soft bread crumbs in milk until they swell. Add egg and salt to meat. Combine with soaked bread crumbs. Form into small balls. Brown in hot bacon fat in a skillet, adding only one third of the balls at a time so as not to crowd them. Remove as they brown to a bowl or plate.

When all meat balls are brown, add minced garlic, onion, and parsley to fat. Stir to mix thoroughly. Meantime, cover mushrooms with water, add salt, and bring to a boil. Simmer 5 minutes. Add mushrooms and mushroom liquor to skillet, then add Worcestershire. Simmer another 5 minutes. Add cornstarch, softening it with a little cold water to make a thin paste. Simmer sauce a few minutes longer. Return meat balls to sauce.

Meantime, cook 1 cup rice in the usual way, to make 3 cups cooked rice. Grease a casserole, and lay the rice in it, over the bottom and around the sides. Put the meat balls and sauce into this. Cover. Place in a cold oven. *After guests have arrived,* turn on oven to 350°F. and bake 30 minutes.

STEP 2: Prepare dessert.

APRICOT DELIGHT	Cheese cake
	1 small can apricots
	½ cup sugar
	¼ teaspoon almond extract

Buy a small cheese cake. Drain the apricots, remove stones, and arrange apricot halves over the top of the cheese cake. Measure 1 cup of the apricot sirup from the can, add the sugar and almond extract. Boil sirup until it forms a sheet from the spoon. This forms a glaze, which is poured over the apricots on the cake.

STEP 3: Prepare the cocktail appetizers. A very excellent appetizer is

MARINATED	½ pound fresh shrimp
GRILLED SHRIMP	3 tablespoons olive oil
	1 or 2 tablespoons minced parsley
	½ teaspoon tarragon
	½ teaspoon salt

Shell and de-vein the shrimp. Marinate in the olive oil, herbs, and salt. *After guests have arrived,* place the shrimp on the broiler rack and broil 5 minutes, or until pink. Serve hot, to be speared with toothpicks.

STEP 4: Wash salad greens. Cut into serving portions. Store in refrigerator. Make French dressing, adding finely chopped chives and finely chopped parsley. Within the hour before guests are due, quarter the tomatoes, combine with lettuce and dressing in garlic-rubbed bowl. Keep salad bowl in refrigerator until ready to put on the table.

STEP 5: Set table. Prepare coffee, ready to cook. Get dressed. Relax.

STEP 6: After people have come, turn on oven. Slip marinated shrimp under broiler. Enjoy these and the cocktails while the meat ball casserole is heating in the oven.

☆ Chicken in the Pot

MENU

Cocktail Appetizers
Barbecued Chicken
Potato Salad   Broiled Tomatoes
Corn on Cob
Celery   Radishes
Frosted Strawberries   Coffee

FOR TWELVE

On a hot midsummer evening, barbecued chicken tastes wonderful. It is light, zesty, the sort of thing you enjoy eating with your fingers. And it's easier by far to prepare than fried chicken.

For winter evenings it's good, too, but for a cold-weather meal, omit potato salad from the above menu and substitute corn pudding for corn on the cob.

STEP 1: Hours beforehand, make

POTATO SALAD

8 medium potatoes
4 strips bacon, minced
2 hard-cooked eggs
1 tablespoon capers
½ cup sliced radishes
⅛ teaspoon black pepper
¼ teaspoon dry mustard
1 tablespoon vinegar
2 tablespoons oil
1 teaspoon salt
2 cloves garlic
Mayonnaise to moisten

First parboil the potatoes in salted water. You may, if you wish, cook them with jackets on, then peel when cold. However, the salt seems to penetrate better if they are peeled first, and they are less likely to become discolored. While potatoes are cooking, fry the bacon. Place it on paper towel to drain. When cold, break into bits. Eggs can also be cooking at the same time as the potatoes. Now crush garlic in a large mixing bowl, rubbing until only shreds remain. Remove these. When potatoes are cooked, chop up into small pieces, add to garlic-flavored bowl. Immediately add oil, vinegar, mustard, and salt. Then add capers, radishes, chopped eggs, bacon and pepper. Let stand for an hour or more until cold. Then add mayonnaise to moisten. It will take about ¾ cup.

Chopped raw onion may be added to the potato salad if you like.

To serve 6, divide the quantities given above in half. Use your own taste and judgment to determine needed amount of salt and pepper.

STEP 2: Prepare

SPECIAL BARBECUE SAUCE
FOR CHICKEN

2 cloves garlic, crushed
¼ cup vinegar or lemon juice
½ cup oil
½ teaspoon salt
1 teaspoon horse-radish
1 teaspoon onion juice
¼ teaspoon mustard
2 tablespoons tomato catsup
¼ cup white wine

Crush garlic in mixing bowl. Add remaining ingredients, blending well. Use sauce to marinate chicken, and spoon over chicken while it broils.

This is almost the same as the Barbecue Sauce for meat except that it has a smaller proportion of catsup, and wine has been added.

STEP 3: Prepare the cut-up chicken for broiling. For 12 people you should have 3 broilers, at least, each cut into 7 pieces. Keep thigh and leg in 1 piece, cut wings from breast, chop breast in 2 pieces, keep the back in 1 piece which has been cracked down the middle. (Save necks for making chicken stock to use in another meal.) This will make 21 pieces of chicken. If you want to be sure of plenty for seconds, have 4 broilers.

For a smaller group of people, have 2 broilers, but prepare the same amount of sauce. It will keep, if any is left over—which is doubtful!

STEP 4: Strip the husks and the silk from the corn. Wrap in aluminum foil, first spreading softened butter over the kernels, and dusting with salt. Later, roast in the oven at the same time as the chicken broils.

STEP 5: Clean celery and radishes for serving. Keep in refrigerator.

STEP 6: Prepare the dessert. For FROSTED STRAWBERRIES, clean strawberries carefully, holding in a colander under the cold water faucet, then shaking from time to time so that all berries are washed. Do not remove stems. After washing, return to refrigerator to chill. To serve, dust the berries with confectioners' sugar, shaking the sugar over the berries with a flour sifter. Arrange on a platter with grape leaves forming the "doilie"—or if you can't get grape leaves, use lace paper doilies. For 12 people, you'd better get 3 quarts of berries, for each berry used must be firm and ripe. Have small dessert plates beside the platter, and let people help themselves to the berries from the buffet.

STEP 7: Arrange cocktail appetizers. There is enormous variety in ready-to-serve appetizers now available. Celery might be stuffed with deviled ham pâté (one canned pâté on the market is especially delicious), or with one of the many flavored cheese spreads. The herring salad that comes in jars is good just as it is, or you can turn it into a canapé spread. The one I have in mind is the Scandinavian type of herring salad, made of herring fillets, onion, and spices in brine. Drain the brine, and chop the herring fillets into small pieces. Combine with sour cream and chopped fresh dill. (Dill is a very useful herb to grow in your garden or kitchen window box. It's hard to find in the markets, and anyway it has more flavor if freshly picked.)

STEP 8: Set out silverware, plates, etc., to be carried to the garden— or set table, if you are to dine indoors. Plan how you will make coffee. Get dressed. Relax.

STEP 9: Shortly before guests are due, cut tomatoes into wide slices. These will be broiled at the same time as the chicken. Dot both tomato slices and chicken with butter as you place them on the broiler rack. Dust tomato with salt and scatter a few shreds of tarragon or parsley over each slice. Preheat oven to 400°F. Place the rack 5 inches below the flame or broiling unit, and reduce the flame to prevent the chicken browning too quickly. Very young chickens can be cooked in 20 minutes, but the average-size broiler needs 30 to 40 minutes. Place each piece of chicken first skin side down, and spoon sauce over the pieces whenever you turn them. Broil some of the tomato slices at the same time as the chicken; they add liquid to the sauce in the broiler pan.

Start the first batch of chicken half an hour before guests are due. You may have to fill the broiler rack 3 times to cook all the chicken, depending on the size of your broiler oven. As the pieces are finished, transfer to a roasting pan in the oven and keep warm there until ready to serve dinner. If your oven is reliable, you need not stay to watch the chicken as it broils. Simply keep an eye on your watch and turn the pieces over after 10 minutes under the flame.

Put corn in the oven, wrapped in aluminum foil, 15 minutes before dinner is to be served. This will be, of course, after all the guests have arrived and are enjoying the appetizers. Bring corn to the table still wrapped in foil. Have plenty of paper napkins, for this meal will be largely eaten with the fingers.

MENU

Cocktail Appetizers
Chicken Paprika
Rice   Green Salad
Cherries with Kirsch   Coffee

FOR EIGHT

Save this for a special occasion. It's bound to elevate your culinary reputation.

STEP 1: All the work of preparing the Chicken Paprika can be done well in advance; it can even be cooked, then reheated when guests are due. Or it can be started an hour before people are due, whichever suits your time schedule best.

CHICKEN PAPRIKA

2 3-pound chickens, cut up
1 green pepper, minced
2 red pimientos, chopped fine
1 cup minced onion
2 cloves garlic, minced
2 tablespoons tomato paste, or 1 tablespoon catsup
1 tablespoon paprika
2 tablespoons butter
5 tablespoons vegetable fat
1 teaspoon salt
2 tablespoons flour
½ cup sour cream
3 cups water

Clean and pick chicken thoroughly. Take out the necks, wing tips, giblets, and cover with salted water. Boil to make stock, simmering for 40 minutes to an hour, tightly covered. This stock will be added to the sauce later.

Dust the pieces of chicken with flour and salt by shaking in a brown paper bag in which you have placed ½ cup flour and ½ teaspoon salt. Now melt half of butter and half of fat in a large skillet. Brown chicken quickly. As each piece is browned, remove and place on a pie tin or plate. Add the remainder of the fat and the green pepper, pimiento (from a can), onion, garlic, paprika and ½ teaspoon salt.

Cook in fat until onion is soft. Add tomato paste or catsup mixed with flour. Slowly add 3 cups water. Add strained stock made with chicken neck, etc. Replace chicken in sauce. Cover. Simmer gently for at least 1 hour. The sauce will reduce and thicken.

If this part of preparation is carried out in morning, put aside until serving time. Then reheat. Add sour cream, in any case, just before serving.

(To make Chicken Paprika for 4, prepare 1 chicken and divide all ingredients in half, except that you may need a little more salt and liquid in proportion. Taste for seasoning and use your own judgment. The sauce, when cooked, should be the consistency of thin cream.)

STEP 2: Prepare the dessert. To make CHERRIES WITH KIRSCH, cut black bing cherries in halves, remove pits. Add ½ cup sugar to each 2 cups pitted cherries. For 8 people, you will need 1½ pounds of cherries. Add 2 tablespoons kirsch to the sugared cherries. Marinate in refrigerator until serving time.

STEP 3: Prepare cocktail appetizers. To make this really a special occasion, you might serve miniature grilled meat balls, banana tidbits wrapped with bacon, and cheese-flavored potato chips.

MINIATURE MEAT BALLS

Add ⅓ teaspoon salt and ¼ teaspoon oregano, powdered by rubbing between fingers, to ½ pound chuck or round steak ground very fine. Blend thoroughly. Form marble-sized meat balls, roll smooth in the palm of your hand. Arrange on pan that can be slipped under broiler. Keep in refrigerator until guests have arrived, then slip under broiler until brown, about 5 minutes, turning halfway through so that they may become brown on both sides. Serve with toothpicks.

BANANA-BACON TIDBITS

Cut slightly green banana into 1-inch pieces. Wrap with bacon. Secure bacon with toothpick. Arrange on pan that can be slipped under broiler unit. Keep in refrigerator until after guests have arrived, then put under broiler until bacon is crisp on each side. Remove from oven, cool slightly, so that they can be eaten with the fingers.

STEP 4: Wash and cut salad greens into serving pieces. Store in plastic bag in refrigerator until ready to serve. Add dressing just before taking to the table.

STEP 5: Wash rice thoroughly until water is clear. Place in saucepan. Add correct amount of water and salt. Cover. Place on back of stove, cook just 20 minutes before dinner is to be served.

STEP 6: Set table. Put coffee and water in pot. Get dressed. Relax.

STEP 7: Shortly before guests are due, reheat the Chicken Paprika, adding more water if it seems necessary. Some evaporation always occurs, and the sauce may have become too thick. It should be the consistency of cream.

STEP 8: After everyone has arrived, heat the broiler oven and put first the Miniature Meat Balls, then the Banana-Bacon Tidbits under the flame. Serve hot. As you return to the kitchen to refill the appetizer tray, start cooking the rice. If paprika sauce is of right consistency by now, add the sour cream. Then put salad together, arrange food in serving dishes, and as soon as rice is cooked, call everyone to the table. The plaudits you will receive will repay your efforts.

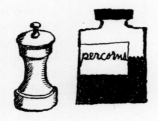

MENU

Cocktail Appetizers
Mexican Chicken with Fruit
Rice   Salad
Guava Surprise Cake   Coffee

FOR SIX

Another super special. Save it for people who like the unusual.

STEP 1: Start the chicken a-simmering hours before dinner, preferably in the morning, because like most stews, this tastes better when reheated. Needs at least 2 hours' cooking time.

MEXICAN CHICKEN WITH FRUIT	1 5 to 6 pound fowl, cut up
	4 tablespoons vegetable fat
	½ green pepper, in chunks
	2 cloves garlic, minced
	1 cup minced onion
	1 small can pineapple chunks
	Few small pieces hot red pepper (dried)
	1 avocado, sliced
	⅛ teaspoon cinnamon
	6 whole cloves, or ½ teaspoon powdered cloves
	1 cup dry white wine
	⅓ cup seedless raisins
	½ teaspoon salt
	¼ cup blanched salted almonds
	2 tablespoons flour
	2 cups water

Dust the cut-up pieces of chicken with flour and salt by shaking in a paper bag to which has been added ½ cup flour and ½ teaspoon salt. Heat the fat in a large skillet. When sizzling, add the chicken, quickly browning on all sides. Remove chicken. Place in a large kettle (a pressure cooker will do nicely, without the pet cock). Now, to the fat in the skillet, add the green pepper, the garlic, minced onion, and the pineapple chunks. When lightly browned add flour. Stir until smooth. Add water. Then add wine, raisins, the hot pepper.

Bring to a boil. Pour this mixture over the chicken. Cover tightly. Simmer gently for 2 hours, or until tender. Cool.

(You may cook it under pressure, if you wish, but I always feel the sauce has more flavor and richness when the meat is simmered slowly.)

Do not add toasted almonds or avocado now. They are added last, as garnish.

Almonds are available already blanched and salted. However, it is less expensive to blanch and salt them yourself. Pour boiling water over the almonds in a bowl. Allow to stand 5 minutes. The skins will then peel off. Now put the peeled almonds on a pie pan, adding 1 teaspoon salad oil. Shake to moisten all almonds. Place in a moderately hot oven until lightly browned. Then add salt.

STEP 2: While the chicken simmers, prepare dessert. To make GUAVA SURPRISE CAKE, bake a plain white cake in 2 layers using cake mix or your favorite recipe. After the cake has cooled, spread the lower layer with guava jelly. Place the top layer over this. Then frost the top and sides with

MOCHA FROSTING	1½ cups confectioners' sugar
	¼ cup softened butter
	2 tablespoons strong coffee
	1 teaspoon cocoa
	1 teaspoon whiskey or rum

Beat the butter until creamy; gradually add sugar and cocoa which have been thoroughly mixed together. Stir in the coffee and rum (or whiskey), mixed together, a little at a time. When the right consistency, spread over the top and sides of cake.

STEP 3: Prepare cocktail appetizers. For this meal you might serve Water Cress Canapés, and shrimps in Tomato Cream Sauce.

WATER CRESS CANAPÉS	1 bunch water cress
	1 3-ounce package cream cheese
	¼ teaspoon salt

Chop water cress leaves very fine. Whip into cream cheese to which salt has been added, until thoroughly blended and very smooth. Spread on melba toast rounds, chill in refrigerator.

TOMATO CREAM SAUCE	½ cup sour cream
FOR SHRIMP	¼ cup tomato catsup
	½ teaspoon salt
	⅛ teaspoon ground cloves
	¼ teaspoon dried basil
	1 teaspoon horse-radish

Blend catsup with cream, salt, and horse-radish. Crumble basil with fingers so that it is like a powder. Add cloves. To serve: stick shrimp with toothpicks and stand around low bowl containing the sauce. Let people dunk the shrimp in the sauce. (Or marinate the shrimp in the sauce, if you prefer, sticking in toothpicks just before serving.)

STEP 4: Wash salad greens thoroughly. Cut into serving pieces. Keep in refrigerator until serving time.

STEP 5: Wash rice through several waters, stirring up with a spoon each time, until water is clear. Measure out right amount of water and salt, combine with rice in saucepan. Keep on back of stove; cook just 20 minutes before dinner is to be served.

STEP 6: Set table. Put coffee and water in pot. Get dressed. Relax.

STEP 7: About the time guests are due, start chicken simmering again, adding more liquid if necessary. Taste for salt, too. Not until everyone has arrived need you do anything else. Then see that appetizers are going around, and slip into kitchen to start rice cooking. Get salad from refrigerator. Remove chicken from kettle to serving platter. Place almonds over the top and avocado slices around it for garnish. Take up sauce in gravy boat. As soon as rice has absorbed all its water, transfer to serving dish and call everyone to the table.

MENU

Cocktail Appetizers
Brunswick Stew   Corn Sticks
White Grapes and Peaches
Cup Cakes   Coffee

FOR EIGHT

This is for the home folks. Good for a family reunion.

STEP 1: Make cup cakes, using a prepared cake mix or your favorite recipe. Frost or leave plain, as you prefer.

STEP 2: At least 2 hours before the guests are due (or, in the morning, if that's easier for you), start the

BRUNSWICK STEW

1 plump chicken or fowl, 4 to 5 pounds
3 to 4 tablespoons bacon fat
½ cup chopped onion
3 cups water
1 teaspoon salt
5 or 6 tomatoes, peeled (or 2 No. 2½ cans tomatoes)
½ cup okra, cut fine (optional)
1 bay leaf
1 box frozen limas
1 small can kernel corn
1 teaspoon Worcestershire sauce

The fowl (butcher's name for a plump hen) should be cut in pieces. Dust with flour and salt, then brown in sizzling-hot bacon fat. Place on paper towel to drain off excess fat. Then place chicken in a heavy stewpot. Cover it with water, add salt, chopped onion, tomatoes, okra, bay leaf, and Worcestershire. Simmer 1½ to 2 hours. Won't be harmed if it simmers an hour longer. Save limas and corn to add during last 5 minutes of cooking, after guests have arrived.

STEP 3: Prepare cocktail appetizers. Since salad is not planned for this meal, use raw vegetables for the appetizers: celery stuffed with garlic cheese, carrot sticks, Radish Butter canapés.

STEP 4: Prepare the dessert, WHITE GRAPES AND PEACHES. One hour

68

before the scheduled dinner hour, slice 1½ cups seedless white grapes in half. Peel and slice 6 medium peaches. Combine the two in dessert dishes. Cover liberally with sugar and add a few drops of lemon juice to prevent the peaches from turning brown. Or pour ½ cup dry white wine over the fruit for the same purpose. (To serve 4, divide these quantities exactly in half.)

STEP 5: Within the last hour before dinner, mix batter for corn sticks —or, if you have no corn stick molds, make corn muffins. Use a prepared mix or your favorite recipe. Be sure molds are very well greased, or corn will stick. Keep in warm place until guests have all arrived. Then pop into preheated oven, 400°F., for 15 to 20 minutes. Serve hot. Have plenty of butter on the table.

STEP 6: After you have everything under way, the stew a-simmer, the muffins in their tins, and the table set, get yourself dressed and pretty. Don't worry about adding the limas and corn to the stew until just before taking up the meal. Vegetables always have more flavor if briefly cooked.

STEP 7: When everyone is at the table, serve up the stew in soup plates. Bring on the hot muffins.

MENU

Cocktail Appetizers
Chicken Cacciatora
Rice or Spaghetti   Green Salad
Baked Cherry Heering Custard   Coffee

FOR EIGHT

Brought down to fundamentals, Chicken Cacciatora is simply chicken with spaghetti sauce. "Cacciatora" means "hunter's style." The adjective is generic. Are there any two hunters who agree on how to cook their game? Use your imagination when you put together your own "cacciatora" and keep on adding condiments until you are satisfied with the flavor.

STEP 1: Prepare the dessert well ahead of time. Custard must be thoroughly chilled.

BAKED CHERRY	3 cups milk
HEERING CUSTARD	⅓ cup sugar
	¼ teaspoon vanilla
	⅛ teaspoon salt
	3 eggs
	1½ tablespoons Cherry Heering

Heat the milk in the top of a double boiler. Add sugar and salt to the milk while it is heating. Meantime, beat the eggs until frothy. Slowly, very slowly, add the hot milk, a tablespoonful at a time at first, blending into the beaten eggs. Add the vanilla and Cherry Heering. Pour into individual molds which have been very lightly greased. Bake at 325°F. until a knife inserted in the custard comes out clean. This will take an hour or more. Don't worry if the knife is coated the first two or three tries. The custard won't be harmed. Better to bake too slowly rather than too fast.

Remove custard from the oven when done, cool, and place in refrigerator until shortly before guests are due. Then take out, let stand a few minutes, and remove from mold. Return to refrigerator unmolded and keep chilled until ready to serve. (If you make the custard in attractive Pyrex molds, or custard cups, there is no reason why you have to unmold them, just bring them to the table as they are.) When ready to bring to the table, spoon 1 teaspoon Cherry Heering over the top of each custard.

Other liqueurs may be used in the same way. Grand Marnier, for example, or Benedictine. Or even sherry.

For a smaller number of persons, use 2 cups of milk, 2 eggs, ¼ cup sugar, ½ teaspoon vanilla. This makes 5 servings.

STEP 2: Either the preceding morning, or an hour before guests are due, prepare

CHICKEN CACCIATORA

2 young 3-pound chickens
¼ cup olive oil, or vegetable fat
½ cup minced onion
½ green pepper, minced
2 slices pimiento, chopped
2 cups canned tomatoes
1 teaspoon salt
1 teaspoon horse-radish
1 bay leaf, crumbled
½ teaspoon oregano

The chicken should be cut in pieces. Separate the necks, wing tips, and giblets from the rest, and simmer in salted water to make a stock. This will be used in the sauce later. Now add fat to a large skillet and heat to sizzling. Dust the chicken with flour and salt, and brown quickly in the hot fat. Remove, drain on paper towel. Add the garlic, onion, green pepper, pimiento, and the remaining ½ teaspoon salt to the fat. Brown the vegetables lightly. Add tomato, horse-radish, and herbs. Combine this sauce with the stock, add the chicken, and simmer for 1 hour. Sauce should thicken slightly. Turn off the heat. Let stand until serving time. If the sauce seems too thin then, make a paste of flour and water to add to it for thickening.

(Chicken Cacciatora can be prepared for 4 with 1 chicken. Divide all ingredients by half, but taste for salt and other seasonings.)

STEP 3: Prepare cocktail appetizers. Here's a suggestion:

CRABMEAT CANAPÉS

1 3-ounce can crabmeat
½ cup mayonnaise
1 tablespoon tomato catsup
½ teaspoon parsley
½ teaspoon oregano
¼ cup minced cucumber
¼ teaspoon salt

Carefully separate gristle from crabmeat. Flake the meat. Mix in a bowl with the remaining ingredients. The cucumber should be peeled, then diced very fine, or grated. Taste to be sure the proportion of salt suits you. Serve in a bowl surrounded by crackers or melba toast rounds.

STEP 4: Spaghetti is the accepted Italian accompaniment to Cacciatora. Rice, however, is equally good, and in many ways better. It provides a less obtrusive background for the highly seasoned sauce.

If you decide on spaghetti, select a large kettle for the spaghetti to cook in, and place the right amount of spaghetti beside it. For 8 people, 1 pound is about right. You will cook the spaghetti in rapidly boiling water 10 minutes before serving dinner.

But if you settle for rice, wash the rice thoroughly beforehand, in several waters, stirring to get rid of excess starch. Place in saucepan with correct amount of water and salt, leave covered on back of stove until 20 minutes before meal is to be served. Two cups of raw rice will be the right amount to cook for 8.

STEP 5: Wash salad greens carefully. Drain well. Place in a bowl well rubbed with garlic, then keep this bowl in refrigerator until serving time. At the table, mix with oil, vinegar, salt, and mustard.

STEP 6: Set table, put coffee and water in pot. Get dressed. Relax.

STEP 7: Taste the cacciatora sauce to see how it is. You may feel it needs more salt. If it suits you, wait until guests have arrived, then go out and turn the heat on under it, keeping it at a simmer. Start the spaghetti (or rice) about the same time. Get the salad bowl from the refrigerator and take it to the table.

For dessert, wait until you're ready to bring the custard to the table before adding the liqueur. This, with hot coffee, should leave everybody happy and satisfied.

MENU
Cocktail Appetizers
Chicken Tarragon
French Fries (Frozen)   Peas
Tomato and Lettuce Salad
Pastry   Coffee

FOR SIX

This is as easy as making a pot of coffee, especially if you let the bakery prepare the pastry for you. Easy, but different. It's the tarragon that does it.

STEP 1: Buy or make your own dessert.

If you especially shine at pastry, perhaps you'll want to make dessert yourself. Here's a suggestion:

PEACH CHEESE TARTS

6 baked tart shells
1 can peaches
1 3-ounce package cream cheese
½ cup sugar
Currant jelly

Let cream cheese soften, then whip smooth. Line the bottom of each tart shell with the cheese. Over this place a dab of currant jelly. Place an inverted peach half over the jelly and cheese. Make a glaze by adding ½ cup sugar to 1 cup of the sirup from the can of peaches. Boil until it forms a sheet falling from the spoon. Pour the glaze over the peaches.

STEP 2: Before the guests are due, prepare

CHICKEN TARRAGON

2 tender young broilers, about
2½ pounds each
1 cup dry white wine
4 tablespoons butter
½ tablespoon tarragon
¼ teaspoon salt

Have the broilers cut into 6 pieces, leaving leg and thigh intact. Dust the chicken with salt from a shaker. Melt the butter. Brown the chicken in the butter, on both sides. Cover, turn heat low, let the chicken simmer in its own juice for 20 minutes. Add ½ cup water and ¼ teaspoon salt. Simmer 5 minutes longer. Put this aside. Meantime, add tarragon leaves to the wine. Let stand until dinnertime.

After everyone has arrived, strain the tarragon-wine mixture, then add the flavored wine to the chicken broth. Bring to a rolling boil. Boil until the liquid has been reduced to half, a matter of minutes. Do not add thickening.

STEP 3: Prepare cocktail appetizers. A good choice for this meal would be hot cocktail frankfurters in barbecue sauce. Prepare Barbecue Sauce, adding ¼ teaspoon hot cayenne pepper. Marinate franks in this sauce for several hours. To serve, heat the sauce, serve hot, with toothpicks speared in the baby frankfurters.

STEP 4: You may use packaged frozen French fries, or you can make your own and store them in the freezing compartment of your refrigerator until dinnertime. In either case, remove from freezer and place in hot oven 15 minutes to reheat. Add salt only *after* reheating, not before.

STEP 5: Wash the salad greens. Store in the vegetable freshener, in a plastic bag, or in a salad bowl previously rubbed with garlic.

STEP 6: Shell peas. Place in a saucepan with 1 or 2 pods to help keep the peas green. (Or use frozen peas if you wish, following directions on package.)

STEP 7: Set the table. Put coffee and water in pot. Get yourself dressed. Relax.

STEP 8: When you are mixing cocktails for your guests, heat the cocktail frankfurters in their sauce. Let the guests enjoy these while you put the finishing touches on dinner. Put peas on to cook. Place the frozen French fries in a pie tin and heat 15 minutes in oven. Add the tarragon-flavored wine to the chicken. Bring sauce to a boil, reduce liquid to half. Meantime, rub salad bowl with crushed garlic (if you haven't previously done this) and mix the salad together.

By the time peas are cooked and potatoes hot and crisp, you can take everything to the table and tell your company to come have it.

74

MENU

Cocktail Appetizers
Chicken with Grapes and Wine
Rice   Broccoli
Water Cress and Tomatoes
Brown Betty Pudding with Hard Sauce
Coffee

FOR SIX

Delicate, different. This is likely to become one of your favorites.

STEP 1: Start preparation for

CHICKEN WITH GRAPES AND WINE	1 3½-pound fryer, or 2 2-pound broilers

¾ teaspoon salt
3 tablespoons butter
2 cups seedless white grapes
2 tablespoons minced onion
¾ cup dry white wine
¼ cup water

Melt butter in a skillet. Add cut-up pieces of chicken which have been lightly salted; brown quickly in the butter. Add whole grapes and the minced onion to the butter. Stir until lightly browned. Then add wine and ¼ cup water, turn up heat, and bring to a boil, reducing liquid. Transfer chicken to a casserole. Add liquid from skillet, along with grapes and onion. Cover. Place in cold oven.

After first guests have arrived, turn on oven to 375°F. Bake chicken for 40 minutes.

(The chicken can be reheated in a casserole or earthenware pot on top of the stove, if that is easier for you. Twenty minutes' cooking time will be enough.)

(If you want to introduce a dramatic touch to the meal, try flaming this dish. Just before you bring the casserole to the table, gently lower a large spoonful of brandy into the hot sauce. Light a match to the brandy as it touches the sauce. A flame will spring up, dancing over the chicken. Carry the casserole triumphantly to the table, which should be lit only by candlelight.)

STEP 2: Prepare the dessert:

BROWN BETTY

4 tablespoons melted butter
2 cups graham cracker crumbs
¼ teaspoon nutmeg
2 cups sliced apples
½ cup sugar
½ cup water
1 lemon, rind and juice
¼ teaspoon cinnamon

Mix butter with the cracker crumbs. Spread one third of this mixture over the bottom of a buttered baking dish. Next arrange sliced apples in a layer, cover the apple slices with the sugar and spices mixed together. Add another layer of crumbs, more apples, and top with crumbs. Pour over all the water which has been mixed with the lemon rind and juice.

Place this baking dish in the oven, on a shelf below the casserole. Baking time is almost exactly the same. Only difference is that the cover should be removed from the Brown Betty during the last 10 minutes, to permit the crumbs to brown slightly. With the pudding, serve

HARD SAUCE

Cream ⅓ cup butter with 1 cup sugar. Add I teaspoon vanilla, or brandy, or bourbon. Keep in refrigerator until serving time, then pass at table to be used on hot pudding.

STEP 3: Prepare cocktail appetizers. A Roquefort-cream cheese dunk for potato chips or pretzels would be good with this meal, and then you can save out the liver from the chicken to have

CHICKEN LIVERS IN BACON

Cut the liver into small pieces, each a little larger than your thumbnail. Wrap the uncooked liver with bacon, cut just large enough to cover each piece of liver. Secure with toothpicks. Place on broiler rack. After guests have arrived, turn on the broiler and broil the livers just long enough for the bacon to be browned and crisp on both sides. (You can, of course, buy chicken livers. A quarter pound of them would be plenty to serve as many as 8 people.)

STEP 4: Wash rice through several waters, until water is clear. Measure in a saucepan correct amount of salt and water. Cover. Leave on back of stove until 20 minutes before meal is to be served.

STEP 5: Cut broccoli into small pieces. Peel outer stem, cut stem as small as you do Frenched green beans. Add salt and about ¾ cup water. Cover. Turn on heat to cook about 10 minutes before dinner is to be served.

STEP 6: Wash water cress. Keep in the vegetable freshener or a plastic bag until serving time. To serve, add water cress to bowl already rubbed with crushed garlic, along with quartered tomatoes. Use as dressing ½ tablespoon lemon juice, ½ teaspoon salt, ¼ teaspoon dry mustard, 1 teaspoon sugar, 1½ to 2 tablespoons oil.

STEP 7: Set table. Get dressed. Relax.

STEP 8: After first guests have arrived, turn on oven. Broil livers in bacon until crisp on both sides. After these have been enjoyed, excuse yourself, go to the kitchen, and start the rice. Remove the cover from the Brown Betty in the oven. Put the salad together. Start the broccoli.

Rice and broccoli should be finished about the same time, if you have timed the start of the broccoli 10 minutes after starting the rice. Now, if you've decided to flame the chicken, remove the casserole from the oven and carefully lower the spoon containing brandy into the hot sauce. Hold it there as you light the match. The dancing flames are a pretty sight to see.

Veal for a Tardy Meal

MENU

Cocktail Appetizers
Veal Escalopes au Fromage
French Fries, Frozen   Petit Pois à la Francaise
Cucumbers-Tomatoes Vinaigrette
Chocolate Cake with Almonds   Coffee

FOR SIX

Reserve this for people who really appreciate the finer things of life. It's superb.

STEP 1: Prepare the dessert. Bake chocolate cake in 2 layers, using any standard recipe or a prepared cake mix. While the cake is in the oven, blanche almonds by pouring boiling water over them, letting them stand for 5 minutes, then removing skins. Toast in oven until lightly browned.

After the cake has been removed from the oven and is cool, spread half the following frosting between the layers:

CHOCOLATE FROSTING

1 package chocolate pudding mix
¼ cup melted margarine
½ teaspoon vanilla
¼ cup milk
1 cup sifted confectioners' sugar

Add milk and melted margarine to pudding mix. Bring to a boil over medium heat, stirring constantly. Boil 1 minute. Cool. Blend in 1 cup sugar and the vanilla. Spread one half over bottom layer at once. Over the layer of frosting, sprinkle part of the crushed, toasted almonds. Place the top layer of cake on this. Then over the top of the cake spread:

WHITE CONFECTIONERS' FROSTING	1 egg white ½ cup confectioners' sugar ¼ teaspoon vanilla

Beat the egg white until stiff. Add the sugar gradually, continuing to beat until smooth. Blend in vanilla last. Work fast in spreading it, for it hardens quickly.

Around the sides of the cake, spread the remaining chocolate frosting. Use the rest of the toasted almonds to garnish the white frosting on top.

STEP 2: Prepare your own French fries, slicing the potatoes very thin. Fry in deep fat; remove, drain on paper towel. Do not add salt. Wrap in aluminum foil. Place in freezing compartment of your refrigerator. Remove from the freezing compartment shortly before guests are due. Reheat in oven 15 minutes before dinner is to be served, and add salt then. (Or you can, of course, buy ready-frozen French fries, though these never seem as fresh and crisp to me as the homemade ones.)

STEP 3: Prepare the first part of

VEAL ESCALOPES AU FROMAGE	6 individual veal cutlets 6 tablespoons butter ½ teaspoon salt Few grains black pepper 3 tablespoons sherry ¼ pound Swiss or Gruyère cheese, sliced very thin

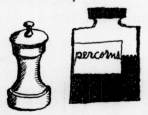

BÉCHAMEL SAUCE

2 tablespoons butter
1 tablespoon flour
½ teaspoon salt
Dash nutmeg
¾ cup milk
½ cup water
1 bouillon cube

The cutlets need to be pounded mercilessly to break down the tissue. Sometimes a good butcher will do this for you. You can do it yourself, however, with the edge of an old saucer or plate. Place each cutlet on a wooden board. Pound the plate edge over every inch of the cutlet, on both sides. Then dust with salt and pepper, and pound some more. (I have been pounding cutlets and round steak this way for years, and have yet to break a dish in the process. However, if you hesitate to use this method, there are gadgets available for pounding cutlets which you can buy.)

Next, melt butter in a large skillet, and brown the cutlets individually until golden on either side. Transfer to a long, low baking dish. Then scrape up every bit of the gelatinous residue in the skillet, adding a little water, and boiling up to loosen. Add sherry. Pour all of this essence over the cutlets in the baking dish.

Make the Béchamel Sauce in a double boiler. Béchamel is essentially the same as "cream sauce." Meat stock is usually added (a fairly good substitute for meat stock is a bouillon cube dissolved in water), sometimes an egg yolk is stirred in, and usually there is a dash of nutmeg. Make the sauce exactly as you would cream sauce. When smooth, pour over the cutlets. Arrange thin slices of cheese on the top. Place in cold oven. This part of the preparation may be completed as long as 6 hours in advance, or only 1 hour in advance, whichever suits you. You will turn on the oven to finish the cooking after everyone has arrived.

STEP 4: Prepare cocktail appetizers. Marinated Grilled Shrimp would be excellent as a prelude to this meal. They serve as a first course which can be eaten in the living room while you complete last-minute steps in the kitchen.

STEP 5: As an added attraction to a very wonderful meal, prepare

PETIT POIS	1 can tiny peas
À LA FRANCAISE	3 or 4 small white onions
	4 tablespoons butter
	Boston lettuce
	1 teaspoon sugar

Use very small onions, about ½ inch in diameter. Those any larger than this should be cut in half. Melt butter in a skillet or copper saucepan. (You may use half butter and half margarine for economy.) Add the peeled onions to the butter. Cover. Simmer 10 minutes. Drain the peas. Add sugar. Add to the butter and onion. Spread a layer or two of Boston lettuce leaves over the peas. (Only Boston lettuce will do; don't try to substitute any other kind.) Cover tightly. Simmer about 15 minutes. Most of the lettuce will disintegrate. Leave on back of stove until ready to serve dinner. Then carefully remove any lettuce that may be left on the top, and heat through—just. Do not bring to a boil.

STEP 6: Not more than an hour before you expect to serve dinner, slice the cucumbers wafer-thin, for CUCUMBERS-TOMATOES VINAIGRETTE. Slice the tomatoes, and arrange both together in a low, wide serving dish with French dressing. Scatter minced parsley over the top.

STEP 7: Set table. Put coffee and water in pot. Get dressed.

STEP 8: After guests have all arrived, turn on oven to finish cooking the Veal Escalopes au Fromage. Grill shrimp at the same time. Reheat French fries in oven. Reheat peas. This is food to be thoroughly enjoyed.

MENU

Cocktail Appetizers
Veal Cutlets with Sherry
Rice   Spinach with Lemon
Salad of Lettuce, Sliced Eggs, Olives
Strawberries in Wine   Coffee

FOR FOUR

A meal that lends itself to an intimate evening. Candlelight on the table. Gentle conversation. Food simple, yet perfectly seasoned.

STEP 1: Prepare cocktail appetizers. Excellent with this meal would be Lobster Salad Canapés, and perhaps stuffed celery as well.

STEP 2. Hard-cook 1 egg for the salad. Cool and peel. Wash lettuce, cut into serving pieces, store in refrigerator in plastic bag. Make dressing of fresh lemon juice, oil, salt, pepper, few shreds of oregano. Slice egg and a few stuffed olives and add dressing to salad just before bringing it to the table.

STEP 3: If you are using fresh spinach, wash it through at least 5 waters. Even the packaged spinach which has presumably already been cleaned needs washing through at least 1 water. Drain. Add salt but no additional water. Keep in tightly covered kettle until 5 minutes before dinner is to be served, then cook briefly in water that clings to leaves from washing. Drain in a colander or sieve, chopping with a knife as you drain. Add plenty of butter and a few drops of lemon juice.

STEP 4: Wash rice through several waters, stirring up with spoon until water is clear. Measure in a saucepan with salt and water. Keep on back of stove until 20 minutes before dinner is to be served.

STEP 5: Prepare the dessert. For STRAWBERRIES IN WINE, clean strawberries thoroughly. Remove stems. Slice. Add sugar. Keep in the refrigerator until about the time guests are due. Then add dry red wine (Burgundy, claret, or red Bordeaux), 1 cup of wine to 3 cups of berries. Do not return to refrigerator after wine has been added. (You can do the same thing to frozen strawberries, but first drain some of the juice. You should have about an equal quantity of wine and berry juice.)

STEP 6: Pound the cutlets, allowing one to a person. Dust flour, salt, and black pepper over each cutlet, on each side, as you pound them. You will not start to cook the cutlets until all the guests have arrived.

STEP 7: Set table. Put coffee and water in pot. Get dressed. Relax.

STEP 8: As guests are sipping their cocktails and enjoying the appetizers, go into the kitchen to cook the VEAL CUTLETS WITH SHERRY. Heat 4 tablespoons of butter in a large skillet. Brown the cutlets on both sides. Then add ¼ cup sherry. Cover. Let simmer at lowest heat for 20 minutes.

While cutlets simmer in the sauce, start rice, then put salad together. Finally, cook the spinach. After you have removed the cutlets from the skillet, add a little more water, about ½ cup, to the essence in the pan. Scrape up with a spoon to get all the gelatinous bits on the bottom. This forms a delicate sauce. Do not thicken. The flour previously pounded into the meat should be thickening enough.

MENU

Cocktail Appetizers
Potted Veal
Noodles   Cole Slaw
Upside Down Cake   Coffee

FOR SIX

STEP 1: Start the potted veal well in advance of the dinner hour—the preceding morning, or even the day before. The veal may be reheated in its sauce at whatever hour you wish to dine.

POTTED VEAL

2 pounds veal, boned
2 tablespoons flour
⅛ teaspoon mace
½ teaspoon dry mustard
½ teaspoon salt
1 cup diced celery
2 tablespoons butter
1 cup water
¼ cup tomato paste
1 teaspoon sugar
10 or 12 small white onions
1 can mushrooms
1 tablespoon cornstarch

Any cut of veal will do, but it should be boned and in one piece. If this piece is very thick, slice it through the center. Pound flour, salt, mace, and mustard into the meat with the side of an old saucer or plate, or the blunt edge of a cleaver. Melt butter in a heavy skillet or kettle—the pressure cooker would be fine. Brown meat on both sides. Add water, tomato paste, onions, celery and mushrooms, and sugar. Simmer gently for at least 1 hour, or cook under pressure at 15 pounds for 20 minutes. Cool. Reheat the veal, in its sauce, after guests have arrived. When you are ready to reheat the meat, add 1 tablespoon cornstarch to the sauce for thickening.

STEP 2: Prepare the dessert. To make UPSIDE DOWN CAKE, use either a prepared cake mix, or a standard yellow or white cake recipe. Canned pineapple is the traditional fruit for upside down cake, but canned apricots and peaches are also good, or you might use a combination of fruit and chopped nuts.

First drain the fruit of its sirup. Then measure 1 cup of the fruit sirup, add to it ½ cup sugar, boil this in a saucepan until it just starts to form a thread from the spoon (about 3 or 4 minutes). Cool. Butter a cake pan, or melt butter in a 9-inch skillet. Place the fruit in formation. Pour in the sirup. Then over all pour the cake batter. Bake according to cake directions on package. After taking from the oven, turn out upside down on cake platter. To serve, garnish with whipped cream.

STEP 3: Prepare

COLE SLAW

2 cups grated cabbage
1 teaspoon salt
½ tablespoon sugar
1 to 1½ tablespoons vinegar
   (according to taste)
1½ tablespoons sour cream
1 tablespoon mayonnaise
¼ teaspoon dry mustard

Grate cabbage. Add salt and mix thoroughly. Mix mustard, sugar, and vinegar together, using smaller amount of vinegar at first. Add to cabbage. Finally add sour cream and mayonnaise. Taste. Add more vinegar, if you like. Chill thoroughly.

STEP 4: Prepare cocktail appetizers. You might have Dried Beef Rolls and Pimiento Anchovy Canapés.

DRIED BEEF ROLLS

Separate thin sheets of dried beef very carefully so as not to tear. Use each sheet of beef for a roll-up. Spread with a mixture of water cress, chopped very fine, and cream cheese, with about ¼ teaspoon salt added for flavor. Roll up tight and secure with toothpicks.

STEP 5: Set table. Put coffee and water in pot. Get dressed. Relax.

STEP 6: After guests have all arrived and cocktails are being enjoyed, boil water for noodles. Turn on the heat again under the Potted Veal. When water is briskly boiling, add noodles and cook for about 12 minutes. Drain. Take everything to the table.

MENU

Cocktail Appetizers
Veal Chops in Sour Cream
Mashed Potatoes   Frenched Beans
Lettuce and Tomato Salad
Compote of Apricots and Grapes   Coffee

FOR FOUR

Another exquisitely simple meal. Can be put together in no time at all.

STEP 1: Prepare dessert. For COMPOTE OF APRICOTS AND GRAPES, open a can of peeled whole apricots. Drain the fruit. Combine with large Tokay grapes which have been halved and seeded. Mix 1 cup of the apricot sirup with 1 tablespoon Cointreau. Pour over the fruit. Chill.

STEP 2: Wash lettuce. Cut into serving pieces. Chill until time to serve.

STEP 3: Prepare cocktail appetizers. Here's a good flavor assortment: Corned Beef Canapés, Salmon Pimiento Canapés, and potato chips. If any of the canapé spread is left over, it can always be used for sandwiches.

CORNED BEEF CANAPÉS   ½ cup corned beef
2 teaspoons Worcestershire sauce
1 teaspoon chopped chives
½ teaspoon dry mustard
Mayonnaise to moisten

Flake the corned beef (from a can) until loosened into fine pieces. Add Worcestershire, chives, and mustard, and mayonnaise enough to make a paste. Serve in a bowl surrounded by wheat wafers.

SALMON PIMIENTO CANAPÉS

½ cup salmon
¼ cup pimiento, chopped
Lemon juice
¼ teaspoon salt
Mayonnaise to moisten

Flake the salmon (from a can). Mix with chopped pimiento. Add a few drops of lemon juice, the salt, and sparingly add mayonnaise to make a paste. Serve in a bowl surrounded by crackers.

STEP 4: Peel potatoes. Cut into quarters. Parboil 5 minutes in salted water. Drain. After guests have arrived, add boiling water again to cover, salt, and cook an additional 20 minutes, then mash with a lot of butter, about ¼ teaspoon of salt, a pinch of black pepper, and just enough milk to soften. Beat furiously.

STEP 5: Slice green beans and cut into inch-long pieces. Add salt, keep in saucepan on back of stove until 10 minutes before dinner is to be served.

STEP 6: Set table. Put coffee and water in pot. Get dressed. Relax.

STEP 7: After guests have arrived, cook the VEAL CHOPS IN SOUR CREAM. Melt 1 tablespoon butter in skillet, add chops, and brown lightly on one side. Turn. Cover. Simmer in juice drawn from meat for 20 minutes. Meantime, turn on heat under beans, add boiling water to potatoes. Put salad together, adding quartered tomatoes to lettuce, mixing with dressing. When chops are tender, remove from skillet, add ½ cup water, scraping up all the bits in the bottom of the skillet, boil for 2 or 3 minutes. Then add 1 cup sour cream to the essence.

While the sauce simmers, mash the potatoes. Then you have only to drain the beans and add butter to them, and your dinner will be ready.

86

MENU

Cocktail Appetizers
Wiener Schnitzel with Anchovies
Mashed Potatoes   Creamed Spinach
Viennese Pastry   Coffee

FOR FOUR

You can imagine yourself in old Vienna with this one. Serve coffee topped with whipped cream with the pastry. Put an LP of Strauss waltzes on the phonograph. Dine by candlelight. The atmosphere will be complete.

STEP 1: For the real Viennese touch, see if any of the local bakeries offer Vienna pastries: elaborately decorated small cakes, *dobos torte,* the many layered cake rich with chocolate icing between each layer (which is Hungarian, by origin, but equally well known in Vienna), or strudel.

Or you might try making this

VIENNESE	½ cup butter
APPLE KÜCHEN	1 cup flour
	1 tablespoon sugar
	½ tablespoon lemon juice
	1 egg
	2 teaspoons cold water
	¼ teaspoon salt
FILLING:	4 or 5 apples
	¼ cup raisins
	¼ cup almonds (optional)
	½ cup sugar

Chop butter into flour until very fine. Add salt and sugar. Separate egg. Beat egg yolk, add lemon juice and water. Mix this with the flour-butter mixture, forming a dough. Wrap in aluminum foil, place in freezing compartment of refrigerator to chill several hours. Remove. Divide dough in half. Roll each half on a well-floured board to fit either a large pie pan or a square cake pan. Sprinkle over it the filling, the peeled apples chopped fine and mixed with the chopped almonds and the raisins and sugar. Place the remaining dough over the filling.

Brush the top with the egg white, using a pastry brush. Bake in a very hot oven, 450°F., for 20 to 30 minutes, or until golden brown. (Or, you can roll out the dough in one piece, then press raisins, apples, and nuts into the dough, and sprinkle with 3 tablespoons cream.)

STEP 2: If you plan to use fresh spinach, for the CREAMED SPINACH, wash it mercilessly, through at least 5 waters, making sure all the grit is out. Then steam until tender, no more than 5 minutes. Drain. Chop fine. Or use frozen spinach, already chopped, cooking according to directions on package.

Now make a cream sauce of butter, flour, salt, and milk, in the usual proportions. Add a dash of nutmeg when the sauce is smooth. Add drained chopped spinach to the sauce, and keep in the top of a double boiler until 10 minutes before dinner is to be served, when you will reheat it.

STEP 3: Prepare cocktail appetizers. With this Viennese meal, smoked salmon and Cucumbers in Sour Cream would be appropriate.

CUCUMBERS	½ cup minced cucumber
IN SOUR CREAM	Sour cream
	¼ teaspoon salt
	1 teaspoon chopped fresh dill, or
	chopped parsley

Peel cucumber, chop as fine as possible. Add salt and dill (or parsley), then add just enough cream to bind together. Taste for seasoning. Serve on melba toast rounds. (The smoked salmon may be cut into squares, sprinkled with lemon juice, and speared with toothpicks. The smoked salmon is also good served on squares of black pumpernickel bread which has been spread with cream cheese.)

STEP 4: Peel potatoes. Quarter. Parboil in salted water 5 minutes, then drain.

STEP 5: Pound the Wiener Schnitzel, bread it in preparation for cooking, but do not actually cook it until after the guests have arrived.

WIENER SCHNITZEL

4 individual cutlets, ¾ inch thick
2 tablespoons flour
½ teaspoon salt
⅛ teaspoon black pepper
3 tablespoons sweet butter
1 egg
1 lemon
Bread crumbs
Anchovy fillets

Grate the rind of the lemon. Mix grated rind with flour, salt, and pepper. Lay the cutlets on a wooden board, and pound the flour mixture into each cutlet by turn, using the edge of an old saucer or plate, or the dull edge of a heavy carving knife or cleaver. Keep pounding until the cutlets are less than ¼ inch thick. Then dip in the beaten egg, in the fine crumbs, and again in egg. Put aside.

Half an hour before dinner is to be served, heat the butter in a large skillet. Fry the cutlets, turning to brown on both sides. To serve, place a slice of lemon in the center of each cutlet and press a curled anchovy in the center of each lemon slice. At table, the lemon should be pressed with a fork to squeeze out juice over the cutlet. The anchovy is simply garnish.

STEP 6: Set table. Put coffee and water in pot. Get dressed. Relax.

STEP 7: After guests have arrived, while they are enjoying the cocktail appetizers, fry the cutlets, add boiling water to the potatoes and finish cooking them, then reheat creamed spinach. By the time potatoes are mashed and cutlets ready to bring to the table, your guests should be in fine appetite.

Pork is Patient

Cocktail Appetizers
Pork Chops with Orange Sauce
Rice   Peas
Salad of Tomatoes, Romaine, Cauliflower
Cake with Wine Sauce   Coffee

FOR SIX

Another simple, quick meal. Only the cake and its sauce take much time, and you can, of course, get the dessert from the bakery if you should be pressed for time.

STEP 1: Prepare dessert. For CAKE WITH WINE SAUCE, bake a plain white cake in a single layer or loaf, using any standard recipe or a prepared cake mix. Prepare White Wine Sauce. The sauce will be poured over the individual servings of cake just before it is to be served.

STEP 2: Prepare cocktail appetizers. A spread of CHIVE CHEESE AND MINCED CLAMS might be served with potato chips. Drain 1 can of minced clams, add to 1 package of chive cheese. A dish of nuts, or something else crunchy, is all you need.

STEP 3: Wash rice, measure with salt and water in saucepan. Keep on back of stove until 20 minutes before dinner is to be served.

STEP 4: Wash, cut romaine. Slice raw cauliflower very fine. Keep both in plastic bag until serving time. Wash tomatoes, but do not quarter until just before salad is to be mixed.

STEP 5: Shell peas. Place in saucepan.

STEP 6: Start cooking

PORK CHOPS WITH ORANGE SAUCE	6 pork chops 1 clove garlic ½ teaspoon salt ⅓ cup orange juice 1 tablespoon grated orange rind ½ cup water 4 tablespoons sour cream

Heat skillet. Add salt, then pork chops, drawing out fat. Move chops around to prevent sticking to the skillet. Turn when lightly browned. Now add whole garlic clove, mashing it against the bottom of the skillet with a wooden spoon. Remove the garlic, after the flavor has had a chance to "kiss" the essence. When pork chops are lightly browned on both sides, add orange juice, grated orange rind, water. Cover. Simmer at lowest heat for 20 minutes. Turn off heat. When ready to serve, reheat, reducing liquid. Add sour cream just before taking to table. Do not add thickening.

STEP 7: Set table. Put coffee and water in pot. Get dressed. Relax.

STEP 8: After guests have come, start rice, reheat chops in their sauce, cook peas. Quarter tomatoes, mix with other salad ingredients, and toss with dressing. Between courses, add Wine Sauce to individual servings of cake.

MENU

Cocktail Appetizers
Roast Pork, West Indian Style
Browned Potatoes   Spinach
Lettuce and Tomato Salad
Ginger Sundae   Coffee

FOR EIGHT

Good for Sunday dinner, whether you're having guests or not.

STEP 1: Marinate the roast. Have it ready to slip into the oven.

ROAST PORK,	4- to 6-pound pork shoulder
WEST INDIAN STYLE	or fresh ham
	Juice of 1 lemon
	2 cloves garlic, minced
	½ green pepper, minced
	½ teaspoon marjoram
	½ teaspoon salt

Set meat in roasting pan. Rub with salt. Mix garlic, green pepper, and marjoram. Rub over top of roast. Sprinkle lemon juice over meat. This should be done hours in advance. Allow 30 minutes' roasting time per pound. For a 6-pound roast, this means 3 hours. If dinner is supposed to be at 7 P.M., turn the oven on at 4:30. This gives a ½-hour leeway for late-comers or cocktail dalliers. Still another ½ hour in the oven won't do any harm. Set oven at 325°F.

STEP 2: Prepare cocktail appetizers. Cocktail shrimps in a Tomato-Horse-radish Sauce would go well with the food to follow. These are also good as family fare. You might also have GHERKINS WRAPPED WITH BACON, which are broiled just before serving until bacon is crisp. Secure bacon strips around miniature gherkins with a toothpick.

STEP 3: Peel potatoes. Parboil 5 minutes. Place in roasting pan around meat.

STEP 4: If using fresh spinach, wash through several waters, careful to remove all grit. If using frozen spinach, follow directions on package. Put in kettle or saucepan with added salt. Cook 5 minutes before serving.

STEP 5: Wash salad, arrange in bowl well rubbed with garlic, keep in refrigerator (or keep salad greens in plastic bag until ready to mix with dressing).

STEP 6: For the GINGER SUNDAE, buy ice cream, vanilla or pistachio, and keep in freezing compartment of refrigerator until dessert time. Use candied ginger as a garnish. If you can't find candied ginger locally, use candied orange peel.

STEP 7: Set table. Put coffee and water in pot. Get dressed.

STEP 8: After everyone has come, serve the appetizers, then start the spinach cooking and get the salad together. The roast should have been in the oven roasting for at least 2 hours. Remove meat and browned potatoes to a platter. If the pork was very fat, pour off the excess fat, so that about 2 tablespoons of fat remain. Add 2 tablespoons flour, a little at a time. When the fat-flour mixture is smooth, add water a little at a time, until the gravy is the consistency of thin cream. Add ½ teaspoon salt. Taste. If the gravy thickens too much as it simmers, add more water. It's better if the gravy is too thin rather than too thick.

By the time the gravy is ready and the spinach has been drained, chopped, and buttered, you can call everyone to the table. Carve the "bird" at table.

MENU

Cocktail Appetizers
Barbecued Spareribs
Rice   Zucchini Squash
Green Salad
Pineapple with Kirsch   Coffee

FOR SIX

Have the butcher crack the spareribs, then you score them (cut incisions with a sharp knife) so that they can be easily pulled apart rib by rib at the table. Spareribs should be eaten with the fingers. "The nigher the bone, the sweeter the meat."

STEP 1: Prepare

BARBECUE SAUCE	½ cup chopped onion
FOR SPARERIBS	1 clove garlic
	½ teaspoon salt
	¼ teaspoon meat tenderizer
	1 teaspoon horse-radish
	½ cup chili sauce (or catsup)
	2 tablespoons vinegar
	1 tablespoon lemon juice
	1 tablespoon brown sugar
	½ cup water

Mash garlic in the mixing bowl, rubbing with the back of a wooden spoon until nothing but shreds are left. Add the remaining ingredients and blend thoroughly. Keep in a pitcher handy to use over the spareribs.

STEP 2: Arrange 3 pounds spareribs, cut as suggested above, in a large, flat roasting pan. Pour Barbecue Sauce over them as a marinade. (This can be done as long as 24 hours in advance, if that would suit you. In that case, keep in refrigerator.) Place spareribs in 325°F. oven ½ hour before guests are due. Roast the spareribs for a total of 1 hour. If dinner should be delayed much longer, turn off oven, later reheat spareribs in the sauce.

STEP 3: Prepare cocktail appetizers. Good to precede this meal would be Shrimp Butter Canapés and Hot Cheese Balls.

STEP 4: Prepare dessert. For PINEAPPLE WITH KIRSCH, peel, slice, and core fresh pineapple, then cut into chunks. Add a generous amount of sugar, about ¾ cup sugar to 2 cups pineapple, and 2 tablespoons kirsch. Arrange in dessert dishes. Chill.

STEP 5: Wash salad greens. Cut into serving pieces. Store in refrigerator in plastic bag or vegetable freshener, or if dinnertime is not too far away, in salad bowl already rubbed with garlic.

STEP 6: Wash rice, measure in saucepan with water and salt. Scrape and clean zucchini squash, cut into rings. Place in saucepan. Cover. Keep on back of stove until 20 minutes before dinner is to be served.

STEP 7: Set table. Fix water and coffee in coffeepot.

STEP 8: Turn on oven. Get yourself dressed. Relax.

STEP 9: When appetite dictates, start cooking rice and squash. You might drain water from squash after about 5 minutes, then add a tablespoon of oil, either salad oil or olive oil, and sauté the squash in oil until tender, about 5 minutes longer. Put the salad together with dressing, take the Barbecued Spareribs from the oven, and there you have your meal.

MENU

Cocktail Appetizers
Intoxicated Pork
Browned Potatoes   Acorn Squash
Tomato, Olive, Romaine Salad
Oranges with Macaroon Cream   Coffee

FOR EIGHT

It's a red-wine drunk, as far as the Intoxicated Pork is concerned. The pork drinks up the wine as it roasts in the oven.

STEP 1: Make advance preparations for

INTOXICATED PORK

5- or 6-pound loin of pork
1 tablespoon flour
½ teaspoon salt
⅛ teaspoon nutmeg
¼ teaspoon parsley
1 clove garlic
1 bay leaf
1 cup red wine

Mix flour, salt, and nutmeg. Rub into fat side of pork loin. Place in flat roasting pan. Dust parsley over top. Place garlic clove, left whole, and bay leaf in bottom of pan. Add the wine. (Dry red wine is generally used, but I have found port to be satisfactory too.) Three hours' roasting time is required. Turn the oven on 2½ hours before guests are due.

(For a smaller number of persons, get a smaller roast, but use same ingredients for seasoning and basting.)

STEP 2: Prepare the dessert. A light, delicious dessert is

ORANGE MACAROON CREAM   6 oranges
1 cup heavy cream
1 tablespoon confectioners' sugar
½ teaspoon vanilla
6 macaroons, crushed

Peel oranges and cut into small pieces, being careful to remove seeds and membrane. Whip cream. Add crushed macaroons. (If stale, they can be easily crushed with a rolling pin.) Add sugar and vanilla. Blend thoroughly. Fold in pieces of orange. Pile in sherbet glasses. Chill in refrigerator until ready to serve.

This quantity is enough for 8 servings. For 4, divide exactly in half.

STEP 3: Prepare cocktail appetizers. Here's one that will have people guessing: Calf's Brain Masked in Mayonnaise. If properly prepared, the brain tastes like the most delicious of sweetbreads.

CALF'S BRAIN MASKED   1 calf's brain
IN MAYONNAISE   2 tablespoons sherry
1 tablespoon lemon juice
½ teaspoon salt
½ cup mayonnaise
½ green pepper, minced fine
½ red pepper, minced fine
Few drops lemon juice

Get the brain from a reliable butcher, for it must be absolutely fresh and firm. Soak in cold water for 2 hours. Wash well, remove white membrane, being careful to keep the rest intact. Then simmer very gently for 30 minutes in 1 quart of water to which has been added the sherry and lemon juice, and the ½ teaspoon salt. Cool. Remove from broth. Place in refrigerator for at least 1 hour. Then cut with very sharp knife into small pieces and mix with the mayonnaise, green and red pepper, and sprinkle a few drops of lemon juice over the mayonnaise. Serve in a bowl surrounded by very crisp saltines. Let people spread their own crackers, and let them think they're eating sweetbreads. No doubt they'll enjoy this delicacy the more.

STEP 4: Peel potatoes. Parboil 5 minutes. One hour before dinner is to be served, place in pan in oven with 1 tablespoon bacon fat. (Do not place in roasting pan. They would become discolored by red wine.)

STEP 5: For the BAKED ACORN SQUASH, cut 2 acorn squashes in quarters, 1 quarter for each person. Scoop out seeds. Place in oven in pan of water for 1 hour, to soften tough outer skin. Then pour out the water, and fill cavities each with a dot of butter, a dash of salt from the salt shaker, and 1 teaspoon maple sirup. Allow an hour's baking time. More won't do any harm. The squash may be in the oven as long as the pork.

STEP 6: Wash romaine, cut into serving pieces. Keep in refrigerator, in plastic bag. Place tomatoes and sliced stuffed olives beside romaine. Quarter tomatoes and mix all ingredients with dressing just before serving.

STEP 7: Set table. Arrange coffee in pot. Get dressed. Relax.

STEP 8: Greet guests graciously. Have cocktails with them as if you hadn't a care in the world. There's nothing more to do to this meal than to remove the roast to a platter, then make the gravy, or sauce. If there seems to be excessive fat floating in the roasting pan, spoon it off. Some pork is much fatter than others. Mix 1 tablespoon flour with water to make a very thin paste. Blend this into what is left of liquid in the pan. Add water to make a sauce the consistency of thin cream, after the sauce has bubbled up for at least 6 minutes. Add salt to taste, about ½ teaspoon. Put sauce into gravy boat and you're ready.

MENU

Cocktail Appetizers
Pork Chops Charcuterie
Rice   Green Salad
Camembert Cheese, Crackers   Coffee

FOR SIX

Pork chops prepared in this way make a very filling dish, so that little else is needed to accompany them. "Charcuterie" means literally "in the style of the butcher," and there are almost as many variations as there are pork butchers in France. The following is the "charcuterie" as it was served in a modest Parisian restaurant not far from the Arc de Triomphe where I once dined.

STEP 1: Start cooking the

PORK CHOPS	6 large pork chops
CHARCUTERIE	½ cup minced onion
	1 clove garlic, minced
	4 tablespoons tomato paste
	1½ tablespoons capers
	¾ teaspoon salt
	1 cup water
	½ cup stoned olives

First heat a large skillet, then sprinkle salt over it. This is to draw out the fat from the chops, so that extra fat need not be added. Add two of the chops first, so that they can be moved around to avoid sticking until part of the fat has been drawn out. Then add remaining chops. When lightly browned on each side, remove chops temporarily, add onion and garlic to the fat. Stir until soft. Now add the tomato paste, the olives (either green or black), the capers, and water. Simmer until thoroughly blended. Replace chops in sauce. Simmer 25 minutes longer, tightly covered. Turn off heat. Reheat chops in the sauce after guests have arrived.

STEP 2: Prepare cocktail appetizers. You might have Tuna Fish Pâté, either stuffed in celery or served on crackers, and

STUFFED RADISHES

- 1 bunch radishes
- 4 tablespoons butter
- 1 teaspoon minced parsley
- 1 teaspoon chopped chives
- 1 teaspoon tarragon

Let butter get very soft. Add the herbs, crumbling the dried tarragon between two fingers to make it powdery. To stuff the radishes, hollow out the top, cut a slice off the bottom so that the radish will stand up. Fill the hollows on the top with the herb butter, piling up so that it looks like frosting. Chill thoroughly, preferably inside a closed container like a vegetable freshener, to prevent the radishes from drying out.

STEP 3: Wash salad greens, cut into serving pieces. A mixture of curly chicory, romaine, and lettuce would be good. Add to salad bowl which has been well rubbed with garlic. Keep in refrigerator. Toss with dressing at table.

STEP 4: Wash rice through several waters, until water is clear. Measure with salt and water in a saucepan. Cover. Keep on back of stove until 20 minutes before meal is to be served.

STEP 5: Arrange cheese and crackers on a serving platter.

STEP 6: Set table. Put coffee and water in pot. Get dressed. Relax.

STEP 7: After everyone has arrived and cocktails are being enjoyed, reheat the chops in their sauce, adding a little more water if the sauce seems quite thick. Turn heat on under rice. Put salad on table. Red wine to accompany the meat would complete the French touch. You might also offer snifters of brandy to accompany the cheese after dinner.

Don't Hurry the Sauerkraut

MENU

Cocktail Appetizers
Duck with Sauerkraut   Duchess Potatoes
Green Salad
Baba au Rhum   Coffee

FOR SIX

This is a meal to serve to gourmets.

STEP 1: Start preparing

DUCK WITH SAUERKAUT
1 large duck, cut up
1 pound sauerkraut
1 clove garlic, minced
½ pound mushrooms, sliced
½ cup white wine
½ teaspoon salt
1 tablespoon tomato paste

Combine sauerkraut, tomato paste, minced garlic, mushrooms, salt. Place in earthenware casserole. Arrange cut-up duck over the kraut. Pour wine over all. Cover. Place in oven. Bake 3 hours at 325°F. Cool to room temperature, then place in refrigerator. Fat will rise to top. Scrape off all fat carefully. Return to refrigerator until an hour before dinner is to be served, then put in cold oven set at 325°F. and cook covered until *shortly before serving*. Uncover, and, if necessary

99

turn up oven heat to brown duck. (Ordinarily, it will already be crisp and brown, but with ducks you can't always be sure.)

STEP 2: Prepare the dessert. Baba au Rhum is one of the most famous of French desserts, and recipes for it are endless. The easiest way to prepare Baba is to buy brioche from the bakery and soak it with Rum Sauce (see below), then garnish with whipped cream just before serving. However, the bakery may not have brioche, so here's one recipe for Baba au Rhum which is fairly simple:

BABA AU RHUM

3 eggs
⅓ cup sugar
1¼ cups sifted flour
4 teaspoons baking powder
6 tablespoons melted butter
½ cup lukewarm milk

Beat eggs until light and frothy. Add sugar gradually, continuing to beat after each addition, keeping mixture very light. Sift flour and baking powder together. Add gradually to egg-sugar mixture, beating after each addition. When most of flour has been added, start adding melted butter and milk. Keep batter very smooth. Pour into a ring mold or a round cake pan which has been buttered, then sifted lightly with flour. (Shake flour around pan, then throw out the excess flour.) Bake at 325°F. for 35 to 40 minutes, until firm and golden. Remove from oven. Turn out of pan. Pour over it, while still hot,

RUM SAUCE

½ cup water
1 cup sugar
½ cup rum

Heat sugar and water together, boiling about 1 minute, or less. Then add rum. Blend thoroughly. Pour about half this sauce, a spoonful at a time, over the cake while hot. Pour the remaining sauce over the cake just before serving. Garnish with whipped cream. (The above will serve 6 to 8 persons.)

STEP 3: Prepare cocktail appetizers. Since this is quite a special meal, you might as well make the appetizers special, too. Perhaps red caviar and sour cream for canapés, Radish Butter, and

MEAT BALLS TARTARE
½ pound ground chuck
¼ teaspoon salt
1 teaspoon horse-radish
Few drops tabasco sauce, or
    pinch cayenne pepper
¼ teaspoon meat tenderizer
1 teaspoon tomato catsup

Combine all ingredients. Press together by mashing with a wooden spoon until of paste-like consistency. Form into miniature meat balls to be speared with toothpicks, or you can spread the mixture instead on melba toast rounds. The meat, though raw, is so highly seasoned its uncooked state may not be guessed at.

STEP 4: Wash salad greens, cut into serving pieces. Store in refrigerator.

STEP 5: Peel potatoes. Boil until tender in salted water. Drain. Mash with butter and milk and a little added salt, then stir in 1 well-beaten egg. Place in greased dish. Later, 15 minutes before dinner is to be served, put dish containing potatoes in oven to reheat. Scatter a few dots of butter over top.

STEP 6: One hour before you expect to serve dinner (20 to 30 minutes before guests are due), turn on oven.

STEP 7: Set table. Add coffee and water to pot. Get dressed. Relax.

STEP 8: After guests have all arrived, and are enjoying appetizers, put potatoes in the oven to brown and reheat. Finish salad, tossing with French dressing. By this time, the duck should be brown and succulent.

MENU

Cocktail Appetizers
Spareribs with Sauerkraut
Mashed Potatoes   Green Salad
Oranges in Port   Coffee

FOR SIX

This is a simple meal with just enough of a twist in flavors for piquancy.

STEP 1: Either the day before, or early in the morning, bake the Spareribs with Sauerkraut, to be reheated after guests have arrived. Or, put the casserole in the oven to bake during the last 3 hours before dinner.

SPARERIBS WITH	1 large can sauerkraut
SAUERKRAUT	1 No. 303 can tomatoes
	2½ to 3 pounds spareribs
	1 bay leaf
	½ teaspoon salt

Combine kraut, tomatoes, salt, and the bay leaf crumbled into bits. Place in a large, low casserole. Spread the cracked spareribs over the top of the kraut. (Two and a half pounds of ribs will be enough if they are meaty and very lean; more will be necessary if they are quite fat.) Cover. Bake for at least 3 hours at 325°F.; another hour of baking will do no harm.

STEP 2: Prepare cocktail appetizers. A very tasty beginner for this meal would be Pimiento Anchovy Canapés. They can be put together several hours in advance and kept in the refrigerator.

STEP 3: Prepare the dessert. For ORANGES IN PORT, peel and cut into segments 6 oranges (1 for each person). Place in dessert dishes. Add 1 teaspoon sugar and 1 tablespoon port wine to each dish of oranges. Chill until ready to serve. (Cherry Heering is also good with oranges. Use about ½ tablespoon for each serving.)

STEP 4: Peel potatoes, parboil in salted water for 5 minutes. Drain. After guests have arrived, add more water, finish cooking, then mash the potatoes with lots of butter, a little milk, and a generous sprinkling of salt.

The essence from the sauerkraut forms a natural sauce for the potatoes.

STEP 5: Wash salad greens. Cut into serving pieces. Store in refrigerator. To serve, add to garlic-rubbed bowl and toss with oil, vinegar, and condiments at table.

STEP 6: Set table. Put coffee and water in pot. Get yourself dressed. Relax. There's not another thing to do until the doorbell rings.

MENU

Cocktail Appetizers
Szekelys Gulyas
Potatoes   Grapefruit Salad
Apricot Sundae   Coffee

FOR SIX

This is one of the most famous of Hungarian national dishes, and certainly one of the best. Sour cream, garlic, and paprika added to the kraut make it superb.

STEP 1: Start the sauerkraut hours ahead of time—even a day or two in advance. When you order pork, tell the butcher almost any cut will do as long as the pork is cut into 1-inch cubes, all lean. Do not use any fat.

SZEKELYS GUYLAS

1½ pounds sauerkraut
1 tablespoon vegetable fat
2 pounds lean pork
2 garlic cloves, minced
1 cup canned tomatoes
1 tablespoon paprika
¾ teaspoon salt
½ teaspoon caraway seeds (optional)
¼ cup onion, minced
½ cup sour cream

Melt fat in a heavy kettle or earthenware casserole. Brown the cubes of pork lightly. Add minced garlic and onion. When lightly browned, add paprika, salt. Then put sauerkraut in the kettle along with canned tomatoes. Cover. Simmer gently for at least 2 hours. Sour cream is added just before serving.

STEP 2: Prepare cocktail appetizers. You might have Stuffed Salami and Avocado in Bacon.

STUFFED SALAMI

Cut thin slices of salami into squares, trimming off edges. Place a spoonful of chive cheese in each. Roll over and secure with a toothpick. Chill before serving.

AVOCADO IN BACON

The avocado should be firm, not too ripe. Peel, then cut into small pieces. Wrap each piece with bacon, secure with a toothpick. Broil just before serving, turning to brown bacon on both sides.

STEP 3: In the late afternoon, within the hour scheduled for dinner, peel potatoes and add to the sauerkraut kettle or boil separately. It is better to cook them separately, for both flavor and appearance, though perhaps easier to cook them in the same kettle. If cooked separately, parboil first for 5 minutes, then, after guests have arrived, add boiling water and more salt to finish the process.

STEP 4: For the dessert, APRICOT SUNDAE, get vanilla ice cream, store in freezing compartment of refrigerator until ready for dessert. Then top with apricot jam. Or, you could use apricot cordial as a sauce.

STEP 5: For the GRAPEFRUIT SALAD, mix curly chicory, romaine, and grapefruit segments with French dressing. Wash chicory and romaine and cut into serving pieces. Keep in plastic bag in refrigerator. Use canned grapefruit. Open the can and drain the fruit, but do not add to salad greens until just before taking to the table

STEP 6: Set table. Put coffee and water in pot. Get dressed. Relax.

STEP 7: Reheat the sauerkraut, just about the time you expect people to arrive. Keep it at a gentle simmer. Finish boiling potatoes while people enjoy cocktail appetizers. You can start the water for the potatoes while you watch the Avocado in Bacon appetizers in the broiler oven. Remember to stir sour cream into the Gulyas just before bringing it to the table.

MENU

Cocktail Appetizers
Choucroute Garni
Baked Potatoes   Tomatoes with Herb Dressing
Ambrosia   Coffee

FOR EIGHT

Don't know why it is, but the French names for foods always sound more glamorous. Isn't "choucroute" a much lovelier sounding dish than "sauerkraut"? As a matter of fact, the French touch in the cooking makes it a much lovelier dish, too. White wine is the secret, Alsatian white wine, if possible, or a domestic Rhine wine type as the best substitute.

You can go all out with the "garni." The more people you have, the more variety you may add in the way of meat. Do as you wish, but I personally much prefer dry white wine to beer as the accompaniment.

STEP 1: Be sure to allow plenty of cooking time for sauerkraut. You can hardly overcook it. Start early in the morning, if that suits you best, then later simmer it once again before guests are due, letting it cook until you are ready to eat.

CHOUCROUTE GARNI

2 pounds sauerkraut
½ teaspoon caraway seeds
2 dozen peppercorns
1 medium carrot
1 cup dry white wine
4 to 6 shoulder pork chops
    (or small rib chops)
½ pound smoked sausage
2 pig's feet (optional)
½ pound picnic ham butt (boneless)

You will need a very large kettle to hold all this. I usually use the pressure cooker, but without the pet cock. It can, of course, be cooked under pressure, but I find the long slow cooking draws out the flavor better. First mix the kraut with caraway seeds, peppercorns, and the carrot which has been peeled and cut into chunks. Then arrange the various meats in and around the kraut, with the chops laying on top. It will be easier to serve if you cut the smoked sausage into short lengths and slice the uncooked picnic ham before placing in the kettle or casserole. Pour white wine over all. Cover. Cook at a simmering temperature for 2 hours or longer. (Or cook the day before, keep in refrigerator, and reheat shortly before people are due.)

STEP 2: For the AMBROSIA, cut up oranges, add sugar, chill in the refrigerator. During the last hour before dinner, slice bananas, sugar them, and combine with ½ cup shredded coconut. Combine oranges, bananas, and coconut between courses, and pile in sherbet dishes. (If you like, you might add a touch of liqueur, about 1 tablespoon Cointreau, kirsch, or Grand Marnier to the oranges when you put them in the refrigerator.)

To serve 8 people, you'll need 5 oranges, 2 bananas, ½ cup sugar. For 4, 3 oranges, 1 banana, ¼ cup sugar.

STEP 3: Prepare cocktail appetizers. A very fine quality liverwurst, served as liver pâté, would be appropriate. Remove the liverwurst from its skin and fluff up with a spoon to spreading consistency. Add a little softened butter or cream cheese to bind. Then press down firm into a serving bowl. Or, if you want to be more fussy, follow the recipe for Liver Pâté. But this is better when prepared several days in advance.

STEP 4: You may serve either boiled or baked potatoes with the Choucroute. Baked potatoes are the easiest. The only drawback is that baked potatoes do not hold up well if they stand in the oven as much as half an hour after they are baked through. So if dinner may be long delayed, boiled potatoes, cooked in the sauerkraut kettle, will wait better. Add them during the last hour before guests are due.

STEP 5: Set table. Add water and coffee to pot.

STEP 6: Slice tomatoes. Sprinkle with tarragon or parsley, cover with French dressing, chill in refrigerator.

STEP 7: Turn heat on once again under the sauerkraut.

STEP 8: Get yourself dressed, then relax.

STEP 9: After everyone has had a second cocktail, start thinking about dinner. The fragrance of the Choucroute by this time will have everyone else thinking about it.

Nearly all these sauerkraut meals can be easily prepared by a woman with a job. The kraut can be cooked the day before, and improves with reheating. Potatoes can always be put in the oven to bake while she bathes and dresses. Appetizers can be prepared the preceding day and kept in the refrigerator until after the guests have arrived. As for the desserts, they can always be purchased at the bakery if there isn't time to prepare one at home.

Duck for Dawdlers

MENU

Cocktail Appetizers
Roast Duck à l'Orange
French Fries, Frozen   Peas
Green Salad
Wine Jelly   Coffee

FOR SIX

For this, or any duck meal, your butcher is an all-important person. Getting a well-flavored duck is more of a gamble than getting a truly fresh-killed, tender chicken. Then, too, since duck is so rich in fat, one must always be sure to pour off the excess fat from the pan before making sauce. In spite of these drawbacks, duck prepared with a special sauce is real company fare, and turns any meal into a banquet.

The following recipe is excellent for wild duck, or for Muscovy duck, if you should ever run across either in the markets. "Canard Sauvage à l'Orange," it reads on a French menu, and the suggestion of a savage duck tamed by a sweet orange is as delightful as the piquant taste.

STEP 1: Carefully go over the duck to take out any feathers the butcher may have missed. Duck can be roasted in advance of the meal and reheated in its sauce. It can even be carved into serving portions ahead of time, and since duck is exceptionally hard to carve, this method has a special attraction.

ROAST DUCK
À L'ORANGE

1 large or 2 small ducks
½ teaspoon salt
1 tablespoon lemon juice
1 clove garlic (optional)
1 orange, grated rind and juice
¼ cup orange juice
1 cup dry white wine
½ teaspoon salt
2 tablespoons butter
2 tablespoons flour

Rub duck with salt, lemon juice, and garlic. Place in roasting pan in 325°F. oven. Roast until duck is tender when pricked with a fork (allow 25 to 30 minutes per pound—but a younger duck will be cooked sooner than an older one, regardless of weight, so the only real gauge of doneness is the old fork-pricking method). Meantime, as duck roasts, grate the rind of the orange, then squeeze out the juice. The remaining ¼ cup orange juice may be made with frozen orange concentrate. Melt butter in a saucepan or skillet. Add flour. When smooth add orange juice, grated rind, salt, and wine. Put this mixture aside.

After duck is tender, remove from oven, take duck from roasting pan, and pour off all the fat and liquid in the pan into a glass jar. Place in refrigerator, so that fat will rise to the top and coagulate, making it easy to remove all the duck fat. Meantime, add ½ cup water to the roasting pan, to scrape up all the gelatinous bits remaining—these contribute immeasurably to the sauce flavor. Add this essence to wine-juice mixture. Carve the duck carefully. Lay pieces in a casserole. (If you have 2 small ducks, split each in half, then in quarters. There is so little meat on duck, a quarter is not too much for each serving.)

When the fat has been removed from the essence you poured into the glass jar, add what liquid remains to the wine-juice sauce. Heat to boiling, simmer 3 or 4 minutes, then pour over duck in casserole. Cover. Reheat duck in oven 20 to 30 minutes before dinner is to be served.

STEP 2: Make your own French fries, or buy them already frozen, as you prefer. Your own, which will probably be sliced thinner and will therefore be crisper, can be wrapped in aluminum foil and kept in the freezing compartment of your refrigerator until the last hour before dinner is to be served. The frozen potatoes will be reheated in the oven 15 minutes before dinner. Salt *after* taking from freezer.

STEP 3: Prepare the dessert.

WINE JELLY

1 package gelatin
¼ cup cold water
1 cup boiling water
⅓ cup sugar
1 tablespoon strained lemon juice
1 cup sherry or port
⅛ teaspoon salt

Soften the gelatin in cold water. Add boiling water to dissolve, then add sugar and stir until sugar is dissolved. Add salt, strained lemon juice, and wine. Pour into molds which have been rinsed in cold water and only patted dry. (If using sherry, the color is not particularly attractive, and you might first line the molds with currant jelly heated enough to soften. Place molds in refrigerator for about half an hour so that the jelly will thicken before adding gelatin mixture.) Chill in refrigerator. During the last hour before guests are due, unmold by dipping in hot water. Place jelly on serving dishes. Just before serving, garnish with whipped cream or prepared topping.

STEP 4: Prepare cocktail appetizers. Especially nice with this meal would be

SHRIMP TARRAGON

1 pound small shrimp
¾ cup mayonnaise
1½ teaspoons tarragon
¼ teaspoon salt
Few drops lemon juice

Shell and de-vein shrimp. Boil 5 minutes, or until pink. (Or use 2 large cans of shrimp, well drained.) Crumble dried tarragon between fingers until it is like powder. Add to mayonnaise along with salt and lemon juice. Blend well. Stir in shrimp. Serve with toothpicks for spearing shrimp. (Or place one shrimp on each cracker or toast round, and top with tarragon mayonnaise to serve as canapés.)

If you feel the need of additional appetizers, serve cheese-flavored potato chips and salted nuts.

STEP 5: Since the main course is French, you might serve Petit Pois à la Francaise. These can be prepared ahead of time, then only need be reheated just before serving.

STEP 6: Wash salad greens. Cut into serving pieces. Add to bowl which has been well rubbed with crushed garlic. Store in refrigerator.

STEP 7: Set table. Put water and coffee in pot. Get dressed. Relax.

STEP 8: Enjoy cocktails with your guests. When appetite dictates, reheat French fries in oven, at the same time reheating duck in its sauce, and reheat peas on the top of the stove. Toss salad with French dressing. The meal is ready.

MENU

Cocktail Appetizers
Salmi of Duck   Rice
Salad of Romaine, Avocado, Grapefruit Wedges
Lemon Sherbet with Toasted Almonds   Coffee

FOR EIGHT

This could be served buffet style quite easily. The duck is cooked and carved beforehand, then reheated in the Salmi Sauce. Roast duck until so tender it all but falls from the bone, and no knives will be needed—always an important consideration when people must hold plates in their laps.

STEP 1: Prepare 2 young, tender ducks for roasting. Rub with salt and lemon juice. Place in a shallow roasting pan, roast at 325°F., allowing 25 to 30 minutes to the pound for the larger of the 2 ducks. (For 4 people, roast just 1 duck, but prepare the same amount of sauce. If any sauce is left over combine it with rice and make a casserole dish for your family.)

STEP 2: While duck roasts, start the

SALMI SAUCE	2 tablespoons butter
	1 tablespoon minced onion
	1 stalk celery, minced
	2 slices carrots
	2 tablespoons chopped lean ham
	½ teaspoon salt
	⅛ teaspoon pepper
	2 tablespoons flour
	2 cups (1 can) beef consommé
	1 bay leaf
	1 teaspoon minced parsley
	⅛ teaspoon mace
	2 whole cloves
	¼ cup sherry
	½ cup green olives, stoned and sliced
	½ pound mushrooms, sliced

Melt the butter in a large skillet. Add the chopped onion, celery, carrots, and ham. (Instead of ham, you could use the lean meat of 1 pork chop, making sure every bit of fat has been discarded.) Cook until the vegetables are soft, stirring to prevent sticking. Add the flour, blending into a smooth paste. Then add consommé, salt, pepper, herbs, and spices. Simmer, covered, for 20 minutes. Strain through a fine sieve. Add sherry, stoned olives, sliced mushrooms. Simmer 10 minutes longer at lowest heat.

When ducks are very tender, remove from oven. Take ducks from pan and pour off the liquid into a glass jar. Place jar in refrigerator so that fat will rise to top and coagulate. Add 1 cup water to essence left in roasting pan, and scrape up as it boils to get all the gelatinous bits on the bottom. Simmer to reduce liquid to half. Add this essence to Salmi Sauce.

Carve ducks carefully into serving portions. Put aside. When fat has been removed from jar in refrigerator, add what is left to sauce, place ducks (carved) in this sauce, and put into a casserole. Either heat on top of the stove or in the oven, whichever is easier for you, shortly before dinner is to be served.

STEP 3: Prepare dessert. To make LEMON SHERBET WITH ALMONDS, use a prepared mix or a standard recipe for the sherbet. (If you are afraid of not having enough ice for drinks, order some to be delivered, or keep the defrosting tray full of cubes taken from the trays in which the sherbet is being frozen.) Chop toasted almonds into fine pieces to serve as garnish for lemon sherbet. For six servings you will need about ¼ cup chopped nuts.

STEP 4: Prepare cocktail appetizers. Crabmeat Canapés and Stuffed Radishes make a nice combination.

STEP 5: Wash romaine for the salad. Cut into serving pieces. Store in refrigerator in plastic bag or vegetable freshener. Open a can of grape-fruit. Drain. Save segments in bowl for salad. Keep grapefruit and unpeeled avocado near by to put salad together at last minute. Pre-pare French dressing, using ½ tablespoon lemon juice, ½ tablespoon red wine (or wine vinegar), ½ teaspoon salt, ¼ teaspoon dry mus-tard, ⅛ teaspoon curry powder, 2 tablespoons oil.

STEP 6: Wash rice through several waters. Measure in saucepan with water and salt. Leave covered on back of stove until 20 minutes before dinner is to be served.

STEP 7: Set table. Put coffee and water in coffeepot. Get dressed. Relax.

STEP 8: While everyone is enjoying cocktails and appetizers, reheat the duck in its sauce, cook the rice, put salad together. If the sauce seems thick, add a little water, making it the consistency of thin cream. For the dessert, between courses spoon sherbet into dessert dishes, top with crushed toasted almonds.

MENU

Cocktail Appetizers
Duck with Olives
Rice   Yellow Squash
Lettuce and Cucumber Salad
Strawberry Sundae   Coffee

FOR FOUR

This is easier than it looks at first glance. Especially if you use frozen strawberries and squash.

STEP 1: Start preparation for

DUCK WITH OLIVES

1 medium duck, cut up
1 tablespoon butter
1 cup dry white wine
1½ cups chicken broth, or
    1 12½-ounce can
1 bay leaf
Few celery leaves
3 sprigs parsley
⅛ teaspoon thyme
¼ teaspoon salt
1 8-ounce bottle martini olives
1 tablespoon flour

Ask the butcher to cut the duck into pieces just as for chicken. It's hard to know the age of a duck, but ask for a young one and hope you get it. Heat the butter in a skillet. Quickly brown the pieces of duckling. Remove to a casserole. Add the canned chicken broth (or 2 chicken bouillon cubes with 1½ cups water), the wine, the herbs, and the salt. Cover, and bake at 325°F. for 2 hours, or until duck is tender. Remove from oven. Cool. Fat will rise to the top. Remove with a spoon. This is highly important, for too much duck grease will ruin the sauce.

Make a paste of 1 tablespoon flour and the sauce the duck has baked in, adding a little liquid at a time. Simmer until the consistency of thin cream. Strain. Add the duck to this, along with the pitted martini olives. Put aside. Reheat either in the oven or on top of the stove a short time before serving.

STEP 2: Prepare cocktail appetizers. You might cut the duck liver into small pieces and wrap each one with a piece of bacon—cut to just the right size to go around the liver. Secure with toothpicks. After everyone has arrived, broil quickly in the oven, under the broiler, turning to brown on both sides.

Another good appetizer would be celery stuffed with

SHRIMP BUTTER

Drain 1 can shrimp. Mash the shrimp with a wooden spoon. Mix with 2 tablespoons butter, softened to the consistency of whipped cream, 1 teaspoon minced parsley or tarragon, and 2 teaspoons mayonnaise. (This is also good as a canapé spread.)

STEP 3: Wash lettuce. Cut into serving pieces. Keep in refrigerator until serving time. Slice unpeeled cucumbers paper-thin. Keep them in refrigerator, too. Combine with French dressing just before serving.

STEP 4: Prepare dessert. For STRAWBERRY SUNDAE, buy ice cream, vanilla flavor, and keep in freezing compartment until ready for dessert. Frozen strawberries will stay in freezing compartment until about 2 hours before dinner is to be served, then remove to thaw. Serve berries straight from the package over the ice cream.

STEP 5: Wash rice through several waters. Measure with salt and water in saucepan. Cover. Leave on back of stove until 20 minutes before meal is to be served.

STEP 6: Remove frozen squash from refrigerator a good 2 hours before dinner. Place in saucepan, add salt. Just before dinner is to be served, add boiling water and cook for 5 minutes. Drain, add lots of butter.

STEP 7: Set table. Put coffee and water in pot. Get dressed. Relax.

STEP 8: After everyone has come, slip the Livers in Bacon under the broiler, and when browned, serve these hot. While appetizers are being enjoyed, start the rice cooking, reheat the duck, put the salad together, and cook the squash. A meal worth talking about.

MENU

Cocktail Appetizers
Duck Montmorency
Rice   Green Salad
Pineapple Cake   Coffee

FOR SIX

You can serve this to the boss.

STEP 1: Either the day before or early in the morning start preparing

DUCK MONTMORENCY

1 large or 2 small ducks
½ teaspoon salt
⅓ cup port
1 chicken bouillon cube
1 tablespoon flour
1 cup water
1 cup pitted black cherries
Water cress

Rub the duck first with half a lemon, then rub in the salt. Place in roasting pan. Roast at 325°F. for several hours, allow at least 30 minutes to the pound. Test with fork to see if duck is tender before removing from oven. When done, remove duck from pan. Pour the liquid into a glass jar and put jar in the refrigerator. Most of this will be fat, which will be discarded as soon as it has cooled enough to coagulate. The remaining essence will be used in the sauce.

Meantime, while duck is roasting, make stock of the neck and any excess pieces of skin that may come with it. Cover with 2 cups water, add ½ teaspoon salt and herbs, such as celery leaves, bay leaf, and onion. Strain the stock, after it has simmered 30 to 40 minutes. Save to be used in the sauce.

Combine stock with the essence from the roasting pan, after fat has been removed. Add port, ½ cup water, and pitted cherries. Boil up, reducing liquid. Taste to see if it needs salt. Thicken with flour, first making a thin paste with water, then thin this paste with sauce. Carve duck into serving pieces. Replace in the sauce, in a casserole. Put aside. *After guests have arrived, shortly before dinner is to be* served, place casserole in oven, set at 400°F., and heat for 20 to 30 minutes. Garnish with a few sprigs of water cress.

STEP 2: Prepare the dessert.

PINEAPPLE CAKE

Use any of the prepared cake mixes, either for white or yellow cake, which call for the addition of liquid only (no added egg). Measure out 1 cup of crushed pineapple just as it comes from the can. Add the pineapple during the last half of the mixing, otherwise following directions on the package. Pour into two greased and floured 9-inch layer cake pans. Bake according to directions for regular layer cake.

Turn out on rack to cool. Put together with

LEMON ICING	
	3 cups confectioners' sugar
	6 tablespoons softened butter
	3 tablespoons lemon juice
	3 teaspoons water
	Grated rind 1½ lemons

Let butter get very soft. Beat with a spoon until creamy. Gradually add sugar, beating with each addition. Add grated rind and lemon juice, then add the water a few drops at a time until the frosting is of the consistency to spread. This is enough for spreading between layers and over the top and sides.

The cake will be a little on the crumbly side, and should be eaten with a spoon. The flavor is luscious.

STEP 3: Prepare cocktail appetizers. You might serve Garlic Olives, potato chips, and Shrimp Tarragon.

STEP 4: Wash salad greens. Cut into serving pieces. Store in plastic bag in refrigerator until time to serve. Add dressing at table.

STEP 5: Wash rice through several waters. Measure with salt and water in saucepan. Leave on back of stove until 20 minutes before dinner is to be served.

STEP 6: Set table. Put coffee and water in pot. Get dressed. Relax.

STEP 7: While appetizers are being enjoyed, turn on the oven to re-heat the duck, cook the rice, and put the salad on the table. Then light the candles.

Gone Fishin'?

MENU

Cocktail Appetizers
Filet of Sole au Gratin
Peas   Carrots
Avocado, Black Olive, Romaine Salad
Flaming Peaches   Coffee

FOR SIX

There is no such fish as "sole" in our coastal waters, so what you probably will be preparing is fillet of flounder.

There's a fair amount of work involved in preparing this dish, but it's worth it if you want to impress your guests. They'll talk about the meal for a long time to come.

STEP 1: Two things are important: the fish must be absolutely fresh, and you must have the bones for the Court Bouillon. This calls for a) a reliable fish dealer, or b) a fisherman husband. To fillet flounder yourself is quite easy, because there are no small bones scattered through the flesh to worry about. Score the fish down the back, over the backbone, then slip a sharp knife under the flesh on either side and lift off with a spatula. Put the fillets aside. Put the bones into a kettle.

117

COURT BOUILLON II

Fishbones
1 teaspoon thyme
1 teaspoon basil
1 teaspoon marjoram
1 bay leaf
Juice ½ lemon
½ teaspoon salt
3 cloves garlic
1 medium onion
2 tablespoons butter
1 cup sherry or dry white wine
3 cups water

Peel onion and garlic. Combine all ingredients in a kettle. Boil briskly 20 minutes. Cool slightly. Strain through a fine sieve. Put aside until dinnertime.

Get everything else ready for finishing the dish, but do not do any more actual cooking until *after everyone has arrived.*

SOLE AU GRATIN

Flounder fillets
1 cup fine bread crumbs
½ cup grated Parmesan cheese
2 tablespoons butter
Court Bouillon II

The oven will be preheated to 500°F. On the top of the stove, bring strained Court Bouillon to a boil. Poach the fillets in it for 5 minutes. Carefully remove with a wide spatula or pancake turner to shallow baking dish. After all fish fillets have been placed in the dish, top with bread crumbs, cheese, and dots of butter. Pour over all ¾ cup of Court Bouillon. Place under broiler unit, at least 3 inches below flame. Reduce flame. Leave in broiler oven until top is golden brown.

STEP 2: Prepare cocktail appetizers. Perhaps Garlic Olives and pretzels dunked in cream cheese to which a couple of tablespoons of minced parsley have been added. And then as something to keep people occupied while you finish cooking the main dish, you might have

HOT CHEESE BALLS

6-ounce package sharp cheese (soft)
¾ cup flour
4 tablespoons butter

Let butter get soft. Mash butter with soft cheese, gradually beat in flour. Form into balls. Place on pan which can be slipped into oven. *After first guests have arrived,* put cheese balls into preheated oven and bake for 15 minutes.

STEP 3: You may serve the peas and carrots separately, or cooked together, as you prefer. If carrots are sliced very thin, they may be cooked in a total of 5 minutes' time. Frozen peas take no longer. But here is a delicious way to combine the two vegetables:

PEAS AND CARROTS À LA FRANCAISE

3 or 4 white onions
3 tablespoons butter
¼ teaspoon salt
1 can early June peas
2 large carrots
1 teaspoon sugar

Peel onions. Cut in half. Add to butter which has been melted in saucepan. Cover. Simmer gently for 10 minutes. Scrape carrots and slice very thin, or cut into very small cubes. Add to onion, along with salt and sugar. Cover. Simmer 5 minutes. Add peas, first draining off most of liquid. Cover. Simmer 2 minutes more. Turn off heat. Reheat to serve.

STEP 4: Wash and cut up romaine for salad. Put in salad bowl already rubbed with garlic. Slice black olives in half, removing pits. Add these to salad bowl. Place unpeeled avocado on top of the greens. Keep in refrigerator until time to serve, then peel and slice avocado, and combine all ingredients with French dressing.

STEP 5: Prepare the dessert. For FLAMING PEACHES, open a large can of peaches. You will need 6 large peach halves. Drain the sirup, saving ½ cup. Combine this with 1 tablespoon honey, maple sirup, or corn sirup. Arrange the peach halves in a baking dish, with the open side up. Fill the cavities with the sirup.

Later, *just before dessert* is to be served, place the peaches in a 375°F. oven. Leave them there 10 minutes. Then remove, add brandy (or kirsch, or whiskey), a tablespoonful at a time, to the hot sirup. Light the liqueur as you spoon it into the baking dish. Carry flaming to the table, and keep the flame alive by spooning up so that every bit of brandy catches fire.

STEP 6: Set table. Put coffee and water in pot. Get dressed. Relax.

STEP 7: About the time people are due, turn on the oven. When first guests arrive, slip cheese balls into oven and watch time so that they bake just 15 minutes. Meantime, pass Garlic Olives and pretzels dunked in the cheese. As Hot Cheese Balls are being enjoyed, finish the Sole au Gratin (see Step 1). Reheat carrots and peas (or cook each separately, for 5 minutes, as you prefer). When you remove the Sole au Gratin from the oven, put the peaches in, lower the flame. Keep an eye on the time, and be sure oven is turned off in 10 minutes, though peaches may remain there until you are ready for dessert.

STEP 8: When ready for dessert, remove baking dish from oven, add brandy or other liqueur, and touch a match to it. Pretty as a picture, and becoming to you, too.

MENU

Cocktail Appetizers
Broiled Bluefish
Baked Potatoes   Lima Bean Salad
Flaming Bananas with Ice Cream   Coffee

FOR FOUR

The dessert is the big moment of this meal. The rest is purposely kept simple and sauce-less so as not to steal too much attention from the dessert. Keep it for an intimate evening, though. It's not the kind of thing that can be done easily for a crowd.

STEP 1: Bluefish has a delicate, sweet flavor, so delicious it deserves to be served plain. One large fish should be enough for 4. Plan to broil it. All you need do is brush the cleaned and dressed fish with oil, and place on aluminum foil. Grill it under the broiler after everyone has arrived. The oven will be preheated for the baked potatoes.

STEP 2: Scrub potatoes for baking, allowing 1 to a person. Place in oven. If potatoes are chosen that are only medium in size, and oven is set at 500°F., potatoes can be baked in 30 to 40 minutes—or after the first guest has arrived.

STEP 3: Instead of a green vegetable, have Lima Bean Salad, and you'll have that much less to do at the last minute. For LIMA BEAN SALAD, cook one half of a package of baby limas (break off while still frozen solid, and return unused part in its box immediately to freezing compartment). Hard-cook one egg. Wash escarole or lettuce thoroughly and cut into serving pieces. Clean water cress. Add all to salad bowl well rubbed with garlic. (The egg will have been sliced, of course.) Toss with French dressing at table.

STEP 4: Prepare cocktail appetizers. Avocado-Bacon Canapés would be good to precede this meal. Have some cheese popcorn on the coffee table, too. That's really enough.

STEP 5: Get everything ready for the dessert, which is to be put together at the table.

FLAMING BANANAS	1 pint vanilla ice cream
WITH ICE CREAM	2 large bananas
	4 to 6 tablespoons kirsch, or brandy
	2 tablespoons butter

Buy vanilla ice cream and keep in the freezing compartment of your refrigerator until the dessert course is due (or make your own ice cream in the freezing tray, if you prefer). Get bananas that are very large, ripe but firm. Within the last hour before dinner, slice lengthwise. Keep in readiness on a plate, with the bottle of brandy or kirsch (either may be used) near by. If you have a chafing dish, plan to use it. Otherwise, prepare the bananas in a copper skillet which you will carry in to the table as the bananas flame.

When ready for dessert, you will heat the butter, then lay the bananas in with a spatula. Cook the bananas until just starting to turn golden brown, on each side. Turn the heat low. Add the liqueur. Then, after a minute, light a match to the sauce. It will flame up at once. Don't be frightened; it will soon die down. In fact, you will keep spooning up the sauce to keep the flame alive—or add only part of the liqueur at a time. As soon as the flame dies down, serve the bananas over the ice cream, with the sauce on top.

STEP 6: Set table. Put coffee and water in pot. Get dressed. Relax.

STEP 7: When guests are due, light oven set at 400°F. to start potatoes baking. After everyone has arrived and cocktails are being enjoyed, put the bluefish under the broiler. When fish has browned on both sides, test potatoes to see if they are ready, and serve the meal.

STEP 8: Remove everything from the table before starting the dessert— everything but what is needed for the dessert. Turn the lights low; have only candles burning, preferably. It will be that much more fun to watch the bananas flame. Hot, black coffee, of course, and perhaps afterward snifters of brandy.

MENU

Cocktail Appetizers
Flounder with Almonds
French Fries   Creamed Spinach
Egg and Water Cress Salad
Ice Cream with Jelly Sauce   Coffee

FOR SIX

Simple but elegant. Requires comparatively little preparation time.

STEP 1: Make your own French fries, cutting shoestring-thin, and after frying, wrap in aluminum foil. Keep in freezing compartment of refrigerator until the last hour before dinner. Or, buy ready-frozen French fries and do the same. Reheat in oven 15 minutes before dinner is to be served. Salt after thawing.

STEP 2: If using fresh spinach, be careful to get out all grit. Cook in water clinging to the leaves for 5 minutes. Then drain and chop. Or buy frozen chopped spinach and cook according to directions on package. In any case, make a simple cream sauce, well flavored, and add spinach to it. Keep in top of double boiler until dinnertime, then reheat.

STEP 3: Buy toasted, salted almonds. One quarter pound will be enough. Crush with a rolling pin, or put through a nut grinder. Keep ready in a bowl to sprinkle over flounder just before serving.

STEP 4: Wash water cress. Wash head lettuce and cut into serving pieces. Hard-cook 2 or 3 eggs. When cool, peel and slice them. Combine all these in salad bowl well rubbed with garlic. Keep in refrigerator until dinnertime. Serve with dressing to which you've added a tiny pinch of curry powder.

STEP 5: Prepare cocktail appetizers, or buy attractive cocktail snacks ready-to-serve. Grilled Cheese Canapés would be very good as a starter for this meal.

STEP 6: Buy vanilla ice cream. Keep in freezing compartment of re-frigerator. Meantime, make GRAPE JELLY SAUCE by adding about 2 tablespoons of boiling-hot water to a glassful of grape jelly turned into a bowl. Whip briskly with a spoon until of sauce-like consistency. Keep aside, at room temperature, until time for dessert. Then pour sauce over ice cream in sherbet dishes. (The same thing can be done with any jelly. Raspberry, blackberry, and currant are all good.)

STEP 7: Order 6 individual fillets of flounder. Dust with a mixture of 1 tablespoon flour, ½ teaspoon salt, and ⅛ teaspoon black pepper. Do not cook fillets until after everyone has arrived.

STEP 8: Set table. Put water and coffee in pot. Get dressed.

STEP 9: After the first round of cocktails, turn on oven to heat French fries, turn heat on under double boiler, where you have the creamed spinach, and grill the flounder.

FLOUNDER WITH ALMONDS

Melt 2 tablespoons of butter in a large skillet. Add one half the fillets. Brown lightly on each side, remove carefully to a platter. Melt 2 more tablespoons of butter, brown the remaining fillets. Each lot requires only 2 or 3 minutes. Meantime, heat the almonds by shaking in a small skillet over low heat. Sprinkle the almonds over the fish fillets. Scrape up the residue in the frying pan and pour over the fillets. Serve with a flourish.

MENU

Cocktail Appetizers
Egg Drop Soup
Shrimp Fried Rice   Broccoli
Blueberry Ice with Toasted Coconut   Tea or Coffee

FOR EIGHT

One Chinese dish in a meal does not necessarily call for an entire Chinese menu. However, there is a reason for using the same general idea, adapting Chinese methods and flavor combinations to American foods. Broccoli, in this case, an Italian vegetable, is cut very fine and cooked only a few minutes. The delicate-flavored dessert conforms with the light quality of all Chinese food, though the Chinese, as a rule, do not serve desserts as we know them.

Connoisseurs who have been around the globe rate the Chinese and French cuisines as the two best in the world. The French consider the Chinese their only real competitors for top culinary honors. Both are artists at combining flavors superbly. The chief lesson to be learned from Chinese cooking is speed. Scarcely any Chinese dishes call for long cooking, and most are prepared in a matter of minutes.

STEP 1: Get everything together for the

SHRIMP FRIED RICE

½ pound bacon
2 tablespoons oil
3 cloves garlic, minced
3 medium onions, minced
½ green pepper, in strips
1 pound shrimp, shelled
3 cups cooked rice
4 eggs
¼ cup soy sauce

You will not cook this dish until 15 minutes before it is to be served, but all the ingredients should be prepared and kept ready in bowls. First, mince the garlic, then the onion. Cut the green pepper into thin strips. Cook 1 cup raw rice to make 3 cups cooked rice. Shell the shrimp. Cut the bacon into very small pieces.

Later, *after everyone has come*, you will heat the oil in a skillet, add the bacon, let it brown for about 1 minute, then add garlic and onion, cook 2 minutes. Add the green pepper, cook another 2 minutes. Next comes the shrimp. As soon as the shrimp has turned pink, add the rice. Then stir in the 4 eggs, whipping the rice mixture with a light, deft movement so that eggs are thoroughly blended. Finally add the soy sauce. No more than 15 minutes is required for all this.

STEP 2: Prepare cocktail appetizers. Buy cheese-flavored potato chips, and spread them with Radish Butter, or have the Radish Butter in a bowl to be spread on the potato chips. Pistachio nuts are also appropriate, as are the thin, greenish Mexican seeds which are frequently to be found on delicatessen shelves.

STEP 3: Prepare the dessert.

BLUEBERRY ICE

1 small can blueberries (15 ounce)
1 cup sugar
1 package gelatin
2 tablespoons cold water
1 cup boiling water
½ cup lemon juice (about 4 lemons)
1 egg white

Mash berries through a sieve. Add water enough to this pulp to make 1½ cups. Soak gelatin in 2 tablespoons cold water. Add boiling water to dissolve. Add sugar, stirring until dissolved. Combine with blueberry pulp, add lemon juice, and gradually stir this mixture into the stiffly beaten egg white. Freeze in refrigerator tray, allowing at least 4 hours. Stir once midway through freezing.

While ice is freezing, spread shredded coconut over a pie pan and toast in the oven or under the broiler until part of it is golden brown. Keep this aside until dessert time. Then, after ice has been spooned into sherbet dishes, garnish with the coconut. A luscious dessert.

STEP 4: Cut broccoli into very small pieces. Place in saucepan or small skillet. Cook only a few minutes before serving: Add ½ cup water, ½ teaspoon salt. Cook 3 or 4 minutes. Drain. Add 1½ tablespoons oil. Cover. Cook another 2 or 3 minutes, at lowest heat. Should be bright green and tender.

STEP 5: Easiest way to make EGG DROP SOUP is to open a can of beef consommé. Two cans of consommé will be needed for 8 people, one can will serve 4. Heat the consommé in a saucepan, *just before dinner is to be served*. Break 2 eggs right into the hot liquid, whisking quickly with a perforated spoon. The egg will form delicate shreds.

STEP 6: Set table. Get dressed. Relax.

(Tea goes with Chinese food, of course, but for Americans, so does coffee. Get out either a teapot, or a coffeepot, or both.)

STEP 7: When appetite dictates, start cooking the fried rice. The broccoli can be started about the same time, and the consommé heated. Let the cooked fried rice and the cooked broccoli wait while the Egg Drop Soup is being served. Such a brief wait won't harm foods freshly cooked.

MENU

Cocktail Appetizers
Baked Fish, Athenian Style
Rice   Green Salad
Butterscotch Pudding   Coffee

FOR FOUR

Fish prepared in this way is rich and very filling. Almost any kind of fish can be used: shad, trout, whitefish, whiting, bass. It will be easier to serve and have more flavor if head and tail are left on—unless you are squeamish about seeing fish eyes. In which case, go ahead and have head and tail removed. It doesn't make that much difference.

STEP 1: For the dessert, make BUTTERSCOTCH PUDDING, using a prepared mix. Pour into custard cups. Into the top of each, while the pudding is warm, press 4 whole toasted almonds in star shape, or a single pecan half. Chill in refrigerator. To serve, add whipped cream around the edge for garnish. Other toppers might be toasted coconut or chocolate chips. These would be most attractive *on top* of the whipped cream.

If you prefer the idea of butterscotch pie as more festive, bake a pastry shell, and pour the pudding mix into it. Any of the garnishes suggested above may be used on the pie.

STEP 2: Wash salad greens, an assortment of several kinds. Cut into serving pieces, and keep in garlic-rubbed salad bowl in refrigerator. Make a dressing of fresh lemon juice, salt, pepper, olive oil, a few shreds of thyme.

STEP 3: Wash rice through several waters. Measure with salt and water in saucepan. Leave covered on back of stove until 20 minutes before dinner is to be served.

STEP 4: Prepare cocktail appetizers. For this meal, black olives, the kind put up in brine, Swiss or Gruyère cheese in half-inch cubes, and a large bowl full of Fritos would be suitable.

STEP 5: Prepare

BAKED FISH, ATHENIAN STYLE	1 large fish (see above)
	1 cup canned tomatoes
	2 garlic cloves, minced
	¾ cup chopped onion
	½ teaspoon salt
	4 tablespoons olive oil
	1 tablespoon lemon juice
	⅛ teaspoon black pepper
	2 tablespoons chopped olives

Rub the cleaned fish with salt and pepper. Combine garlic, onion, tomatoes, and chopped olives. Pimiento-stuffed olives are fine, though any kind can be used, including black olives. Pour half the oil in a baking dish. Put the chopped vegetables over this. Then lay the fish on top of the vegetables. Brush the fish with the remaining olive oil. Now the fish is ready to bake, but don't turn on the oven until after your company has arrived. Twenty minutes' baking time at 450°F. should be enough. To make the fish brown and crisp-looking, you might put it under the broiler a few minutes.

The rice can cook while the fish is in the oven. Then everything will be ready at once.

128

MENU

Cocktail Appetizers
Lobster Gratine
Cauliflower with Lemon
Escarole, Egg, Tomato Salad
Chocolate Pie   Coffee

FOR FOUR

The best way to cook lobster, as everyone knows, is to plunge the live creature into boiling water. But I haven't the nerve. Not even to try it. The big African lobster tails are pure meat, easier to handle, and quite delicious. That's what I use.

STEP 1: Well in advance, bake a pastry shell for the CHOCOLATE PIE. When the shell is cool, cook prepared chocolate pudding mix. Pour into shell. Either put whipped cream on top, or stiffly beaten egg white sweetened with sugar for a meringue, baked in a 300°F. oven for 15 or 20 minutes. The easiest garnish, of course, is a prepared topping.

STEP 2: Prepare cocktail appetizers. Garlic Olives, pretzels dunked in chive cheese, and Avocado-Bacon Canapés would be suitable.

STEP 3: Not too long before dinner is to be served, start preparing the

LOBSTER GRATINE

4 lobster tails, fresh or frozen
3 tablespoons butter
2 tablespoons flour
½ cup sherry
¼ teaspoon dry mustard
⅓ cup dry white wine
½ teaspoon salt
1 cup sour cream
2 cups cooked rice
¼ cup grated Swiss cheese
½ cup fine bread crumbs

Heat 3 cups water to boiling. Add the white wine and ½ teaspoon salt. Add the lobster tails, reduce heat to simmering, cook gently for 15 minutes. Be careful not to overcook or meat will become tough. Take from liquid with perforated spoon, saving the liquid. Crack the lobster shells and remove meat. Cool. When cool, slice fine with a sharp knife.

Meantime, make the sauce. Melt the butter in a saucepan or copper skillet, blend in flour. Add 1 cup of the liquor lobster cooked in. Then add ½ cup sherry and the mustard. Finally turn off the heat and blend in the sour cream. Add the slices of lobster meat, being careful not to break them up.

Now grease a casserole, or individual ramekins. Spread cooked rice over the bottom. On this pile the lobster in its sauce. Over the lobster spread grated cheese mixed with crumbs. Dot with bits of butter.

Do not put into oven until shortly before dinner is to be served. Then you will bake it at 400°F. until the crumbs are golden brown, about 15 or 20 minutes.

STEP 3: Cut cauliflower into flowerlets. Place in saucepan on back of stove. Sprinkle lemon juice over it to prevent turning brown.

STEP 4: Wash escarole. Cut into serving pieces. Add to salad bowl already rubbed with garlic. Hard-cook 1 egg. Cool it, slice, add to salad bowl. Wash tomatoes, but do not quarter until ready to serve salad.

STEP 5: Set table. Put coffee and water in pot. Get dressed.

STEP 6: After everyone has come and cocktails are being enjoyed, put the lobster in the oven. At the same time, cook the cauliflower and put the salad together. That's all, for the pie has been ready for hours.

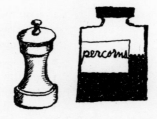

MENU

Cocktail Appetizers
Coquille St. Jacques
Baked Potatoes   Green Salad
Peach Cobbler with Cream   Coffee

FOR FOUR

Light but satisfying. Good for Sunday-night supper, or a reunion with old friends.

STEP 1: Prepare the dessert.

PEACH COBBLER

1 large can peaches, or
   2 packages frozen peaches
1 cup prepared biscuit mix
1 tablespoon butter
1 tablespoon sugar
2 tablespoons milk

Either fresh, canned, or frozen peaches may be used. If fresh peaches are used, sugar must be added to sweeten the peaches. In any case, place peaches in the bottom of a baking dish, with the sirup from those frozen or canned. To prepared biscuit mix, add 1 tablespoon sugar, chop in an extra tablespoon of butter, and add the milk as directed on the package. Roll out lightly with a rolling pin to about ¼-inch thickness. Prick. The crust need not cover the peaches to the very edge of the dish, for if some of the peach juice comes up over the crust, it tastes that much better. Place in cold oven, to be baked at same time as the main dish.

STEP 2: Prepare

COQUILLE ST. JACQUES

1½ pounds scallops
3 tablespoons butter
3 tablespoons flour
2 cups hot milk
1 bouillon cube
½ teaspoon salt
1 egg yolk
⅓ cup dry white wine, or sherry
½ cup grated cheese
¾ cup fine bread crumbs

Parboil the scallops *in their own liquor* for 2 minutes. Then make sauce of butter, flour, heated milk, salt, bouillon cube. Add a little of this sauce at a time to beaten egg yolk. Finally add white wine or sherry. Mix the scallops and their liquor with this sauce. Pour into 4 individual ramekins (shallow baking dishes) which have been well buttered. (If you don't have ramekins, use the shallowest baking dish you have.) Cover with the cheese which has been thoroughly mixed with bread crumbs. Dot with bits of butter. *After guests have arrived,* place this in preheated oven. Bake at 400°F. for about 20 minutes, or until crumbs are nicely browned.

STEP 3: Scrub potatoes. Place in oven. *About time guests are expected,* turn on oven to 400°F., allowing 40 minutes' to 1 hour's baking time.

STEP 4: Prepare cocktail appetizers. Small pieces of banana, wrapped with bacon and broiled quickly, would make attractive appetizers for this meal. Secure with toothpicks, and arrange on pan that can be slipped under broiler.

Another colorful appetizer would be Pimiento Anchovy Canapés.

STEP 5: Wash salad greens, cut into serving pieces, keep in refrigerator until serving time.

STEP 6: As soon as first guests have arrived, slip banana-bacon appetizers under broiler. Meantime, pass other canapés. Peach Cobbler should also be placed in oven to bake, and when Banana-Bacon Tidbits are ready, it will be time to put the scallops under the broiler flame. Place these 4 or 5 inches below the flame, in preheated oven. As soon as crumbs are nicely browned on the Coquille St. Jacques, and potatoes are tender, turn off the oven. The cobbler should be baked by now too. In any case, once the oven is turned off, it won't hurt the cobbler to remain inside, and it should be hot when served. Pass cream to be poured over the cobbler.

Spaghetti for Slowpokes

MENU

Cocktail Appetizers
Spaghetti Omelet
Frenched Green Beans   Lettuce and Tomatoes
Maple Sirup Sundae   Coffee

FOR SIX

Everyone has leftover spaghetti in the refrigerator at times. This is an excellent way to make use of it. And a fine idea for an emergency meal, when you invite people to come have "pot luck" on the spur of the moment without knowing whether there's anything at all to give them.

If you have no leftover spaghetti on hand, use canned spaghetti. The new chili-spaghetti would be good.

STEP 1: Two cups of spaghetti and sauce together will be needed for the omelet. Chop up the spaghetti into short lengths. Keep in a bowl on the back of the stove. Beside it place 4 eggs. Beat eggs and mix with spaghetti only *a few minutes before you expect to have dinner.*

STEP 2: Slice string beans. Put in saucepan with water and salt. Allow 10 minutes for cooking.

STEP 3: Clean lettuce. Cut into serving pieces. Combine with quartered tomatoes in last half hour before dinner. Serve with prepared French or Russian dressing. (To make Russian dressing, simply add a little catsup and about a tablespoonful of finely chopped pickle to mayonnaise.)

STEP 4: Arrange cocktail appetizers in bowls. Pick up a variety of taste-teasers in the delicatessen, or at your own grocer's, such things as coconut chips, deviled ham pâté, or one of the many flavored cheese spreads.

STEP 5: For the dessert, MAPLE SIRUP SUNDAE, buy ice cream: coffee, pistachio, or vanilla flavor. Store in freezing compartment until dessert time. Then you will serve with maple sirup as a sauce.

STEP 6: As people enjoy cocktails, start the beans cooking, put the salad together, and cook the SPAGHETTI OMELET.

Put a generous tablespoonful of butter in your omelet pan. Keep the heat low. Now beat 4 eggs with a fork or wire whisk. Add ¼ teaspoon salt and 3 tablespoons milk. Stir spaghetti into eggs. Pour into omelet pan. With a spatula lift up edges of omelet allowing liquid to run under. Cut small grooves in the center for the same purpose. When omelet is solid all the way through, only slightly moist on top, start lifting for a look-see as to whether it has browned on the bottom. Keep heat low all the time. Never turn up heat to hurry an omelet. As soon as it is golden on the bottom, loosen all over with the spatula, and by shaking the pan gently. Then invert a plate over the omelet pan (do not try to fold this thick filled omelet) and turn the pan upside down, so that omelet comes out with the golden side up. Cut into pie-shaped wedges. Serve without delay.

(There is only one way to prevent an omelet from sticking, and that is to save one skillet for omelets alone, and never, never wash it. Clean by rubbing with a paper towel, using successive pieces of paper until there is no trace of grease left. If some well-meaning friend or relative does put the omelet pan in the dishwater, you will probably find it sticks thereafter. Then the best way to treat it is to rub it repeatedly with vegetable fat, cleaning with paper each time, and, for a while afterward, use extra butter each time before adding the eggs, until it finally stops sticking.)

MENU

Cocktail Appetizers
Chicken Tetrazzini
Broccoli   Garlic Bread
Avocado, Tomato, Romaine Salad
Banana Ice Cream Cake   Coffee

FOR TEN

This will go over with any group, of any age. It's easily served from a buffet.

STEP 1: Start preparing

CHICKEN TETRAZZINI

2 cups cooked chicken meat
2½ cups chicken broth
1 pound thin spaghetti
3 tablespoons butter
3 tablespoons flour
½ pound mushrooms, sliced
½ teaspoon salt
½ teaspoon oregano
⅛ teaspoon nutmeg
1 cup light cream
12 pitted black olives (optional)
½ cup grated Swiss or Parmesan cheese
⅓ cup sherry

Parboil the chicken, a 5-pound plump hen (fowl, the butcher will call it), either the night before or early in the morning. Leave the hen whole or split in half. Cover with 4 cups water to which has been added ½ teaspoon salt, 1 onion, and a bunch of celery leaves. Simmer until tender enough to fall from the bones. Cool. Remove chicken from broth with perforated spoon. Carefully pick off the meat, and break up into small pieces. Strain the broth. Measure off 2½ cups. Use all the chicken meat there is. It won't matter if you have more than 2 cups. This is a minimum.

(Or you can use canned chicken and chicken broth, much more expensive, but easier.)

You will need a very large casserole for this quantity of Tetrazzini —which is my own version of the dish originally named for the opera diva. If you haven't a baking dish large enough, use a roasting pan. Grease it well. Then line bottom and sides with a layer of spaghetti (which has been precooked in rapidly boiling salted water for 8 to 10 minutes).

Now melt butter in a large skillet. Add sliced mushrooms, and toss in the butter until they are well coated. Stir in flour, making a thin paste (add a little more butter, if necessary, to keep the paste fluid). Then add the strained chicken broth gradually, and finally the cream. Season with salt, nutmeg, and oregano. Add pitted black olives and sherry. Now gently stir in the chicken. Pour most of this mixture over the spaghetti. Top with remaining spaghetti. Add rest of chicken. Cover with grated cheese. Put the dish aside.

After guests have started to arrive, put the Tetrazzini into a preheated 375°F. oven and bake for 45 minutes. You can slip the casserole into the oven when you go out to mix cocktails.

To serve 6, use 1 cup chicken meat, 1½ cups broth, 2 tablespoons each butter and flour, ¼ pound mushrooms, ⅔ cup cream, ½ pound spaghetti, 6 olives. The remaining ingredients are the same.

STEP 2: For the dessert, bake a 2-layer chocolate cake, using a prepared mix or any standard recipe. Do not ice cake. Put the two layers aside until time to serve dessert. Meantime, get together ingredients for

BANANA ICE CREAM CAKE   2 medium bananas
Maraschino cherries
1 quart vanilla or banana ice cream
2-layer chocolate cake

Put the ice cream in the freezing compartment of refrigerator until ready to serve. Open jar of cherries. Do not slice and sugar bananas until shortly before guests are due. Then add ¼ cup sugar to the cut-up bananas. To serve, spread a thin frosting of ice cream over bottom layer of cake. Put sliced bananas over this. Cover with top layer of cake. Spread ice cream over top and sides. Decorate with cherries.

You will have to work quickly, and serve as soon as assembled, before ice cream melts. Be sure ice cream is kept very firm, with refrigerator control at very cold.

This makes a delicious and impressive dessert, but of course it must all be eaten at one meal, so it's no good for a small gathering. For fewer people, you might make cup cakes, and frost them with ice cream.

STEP 3: Prepare cocktail appetizers. For a crowd of 10, a variety of appetizers is necessary. You might have celery stuffed with garlic cheese, olives, Curried Tuna Fish Canapés, and Cocktail Frankfurters in Barbecue Sauce. Marinate the frankfurters in this sauce for several hours, then heat in the sauce and serve hot when everyone has arrived.

STEP 4: Cut broccoli into serving pieces. For a large number of people, it would be smart to cook the broccoli in the pressure cooker, if you have one. Only 2 to 3 minutes' cooking time is required after the correct pressure is reached. It's difficult to cook a large quantity of broccoli in an ordinary saucepan and keep it bright and green. If you have no pressure cooker, use a large enough saucepan or kettle so that the broccoli can be cooked quickly without crowding.

STEP 5: Fix GARLIC BREAD. Melt one quarter pound butter (or half butter, half margarine). Add to it 1 or 2 cloves of garlic. Let garlic remain in butter just long enough to impart flavor, then remove. Cut gashes in a long loaf of French bread, at a 45° angle, without cutting all the way through. Spread the gashes with garlic butter. Place the bread in a roasting pan or on the broiler rack, but do not slip into oven until 10 minutes before dinner is to be served. If your guests are the type who eat lustily, better have two loaves of bread.

STEP 6: Wash romaine, cut into serving pieces, store in vegetable freshener, plastic bag, or in the salad bowl, which has previously been rubbed with garlic. Have tomato and avocado alongside, in readiness. Mix French dressing, adding a touch of curry powder.

STEP 7: Set table. Put water and coffee in pot. Get dressed.

STEP 8: At hour when guests are due, turn on oven. When the first guests arrive, slip Tetrazzini into oven, which has been set at 375° F. Ten minutes before you gauge the time to be right for putting the food on the buffet, start cooking the broccoli, and slip the garlic bread into the oven. Keep a sharp eye on the bread; don't let it get too brown.

Between courses, you will frost the cake with ice cream, slipping bananas and cherries between the layers and on top.

MENU

Cocktail Appetizers
Baked Lasagne
Zucchini Squash   Green Salad
Ice Cream with Peach Rum Sauce   Coffee

FOR EIGHT

The chief difficulty in preparing this meal is in finding lasagne. Few groceries carry it. However, it can always be found in an Italian section, and if there is no Italian section near you, just substitute wide macaroni. After all, that's what lasagne is—very wide macaroni.

STEP 1: Prepare

BAKED LASAGNE

⅓ to ½ pound lasagne
1 medium onion, sliced
4 tablespoons oil
2 cloves garlic, minced
¾ teaspoon salt
⅛ teaspoon black pepper
2 tablespoons minced parsley
1 teaspoon sugar
1 cup canned tomatoes
1 cup water
1 bouillon cube
2 tablespoons sherry
1 6-ounce can tomato paste
½ pound cream cheese, or ½ pound ricotta cheese
¾ cup grated Parmesan cheese

First cook the lasagne in a large kettle of rapidly boiling water for 20 to 25 minutes. While lasagne cooks, start the sauce. Slice onion. Heat oil in a skillet (olive oil is best, but you can use vegetable oil). Add onions to oil, cover, simmer until onions are soft. Then add minced garlic, minced parsley, salt, pepper, tomato paste, canned tomatoes, bouillon cube, sugar, and water. Let simmer gently for 10 minutes. Add sherry. Meantime, drain lasagne, rinse in a colander under cold water. If you can find ricotta cheese in the markets, by all means use it, but the ordinary cream cheese will do as a substitute. Soften the cream cheese with some of the tomato sauce until it is of the consistency of thick cream. Grease a large casserole or roasting pan. Place in it first a layer of lasagne, then tomato sauce, then cream cheese, and finally half the grated Parmesan cheese. Repeat, until all ingredients are used. Cover with grated Parmesan cheese over top.

Put the casserole aside until *after everyone has arrived.* Then slip into a hot oven, 400°F., and bake, covered, 30 minutes. It won't be harmed if it stays in the oven as long as an hour.

STEP 2: Buy ice cream, store in freezing compartment of refrigerator until needed. Prepare the

PEACH RUM SAUCE   1 jar peach preserves (¾ cup)
                         3 tablespoons rum

Mix the preserves and rum together. Heat to boiling, boil 1 minute. Cool. Pour into a pitcher.

To serve, take ice cream from freezer, spoon into dessert dishes, and pour a liberal amount of sauce over cream.

(Other variations of this idea: Grand Marnier with peach preserves. Or orange marmalade with Grand Marnier.)

STEP 3: Prepare cocktail appetizers. To precede this meal, you might offer shrimps on Radish Butter, and

EGG AND OLIVE CANAPÉS   1 hard-cooked egg
                         ¼ cup olives, minced
                         ¼ cup mayonnaise
                         Few grains salt

Remove yolk from egg, crumble fine with a fork. Add the mayonnaise and salt to taste. Finally add the olives and the egg white, both minced very, very fine. Serve in a bowl surrounded by crackers, so that people can spread their own canapés.

STEP 4: Scrape the zucchini with a sharp knife. Cut into thick slices. Place in a heavy saucepan, with tight-fitting cover, along with ⅓ cup olive oil and ½ teaspoon salt. This is to be cooked in the oil, without water.

STEP 5: Wash salad greens. Cut into serving pieces. Place in salad bowl well rubbed with garlic. Keep in refrigerator until time to serve. Then mix with oil, vinegar, and condiments at table.

STEP 6: Set table. Put coffee and water in pot. Get dressed. Relax.

STEP 7: While first round of cocktails is being enjoyed, put the lasagne in the oven. Twenty-five minutes later, turn the heat on under the squash, to cook 5 to 10 minutes, or until tender. Get the salad out of the refrigerator, and put on the table. That's it.

MENU

Cocktail Appetizers
Spaghetti-Ham Casserole   Spinach
Tomato-Egg-Romaine Salad
Biscuit Tortoni   Coffee

FOR SIX

Good for a neighborhood get-together. Can easily be served from a buffet.

STEP 1: In the morning, prepare

BISCUIT TORTONI
- ½ cup crushed macaroons
- ½ cup milk
- ½ cup confectioners' sugar
- ¾ cup heavy cream, whipped
- ½ teaspoon vanilla
- Few grains salt

Crush the macaroons very fine. Combine with milk, sugar, and salt in a bowl. Let stand for 1 hour. Then whip the cream until stiff.

Fold the macaroon mixture into it, add vanilla, and pour into paper muffin cups. Place the cups close together in a refrigerator freezing tray; otherwise, they may spread out like water lilies. Turn the control to the coldest point. Freeze at least 4 hours. Leave in freezer until time for dessert. (Double quantities exactly to fill a dozen paper cups.)

STEP 2: Prepare for baking

SPAGHETTI-HAM CASSEROLE

½ pound spaghetti
1 6-ounce can tomato paste
1 bouillon cube
1 cup boiling water
½ teaspoon oregano
¼ cup sherry
2 ham steaks, sliced thin
1 package frozen limas
½ cup grated sharp cheese

Cook the spaghetti in rapidly boiling water for 8 to 10 minutes. Drain. Arrange half the spaghetti in the bottom of a large casserole or a shallow roasting pan. Spread the uncooked frozen limas over this. Cut the ham into serving pieces. (Slices can be cut from a leftover roast ham, if you happen to have one in the refrigerator. Or you can cook a smoked pork butt and cut slices from that, saving the rest of the ham for another meal.) Put about one third the ham over the limas. Then add another layer of spaghetti, and the rest of the ham on top of that. Meantime, add oregano, sherry, the bouillon cube, and boiling water to the tomato paste in a saucepan. Heat until the cube is completely dissolved. Pour sauce over the spaghetti. If sauce does not come to top of dish, add water enough to bring it to the top. Spread grated cheese as a final layer. Put aside. *After the first guests have arrived,* slip the casserole in an oven already heated to 400°F., and bake 20 to 30 minutes, or until top is golden and bubbling.

STEP 3: Prepare cocktail appetizers. Hot appetizers are always impressive, and they are not too hard to prepare.

FRENCH FRIED ANCHOVIES

1 tin anchovy fillets
1 beaten egg
½ cup milk
½ cup pancake mix
Fat for frying

Heat fat to the depth of at least 3 inches in a kettle or heavy saucepan. Test with a piece of stale bread to be sure it is hot enough (unless you have a special thermometer for jobs like this). Carefully lower into the fat anchovies which have been dipped into a batter made of the egg, milk, and the pancake mix. Fry until golden brown. Drain on paper towel. When ready to serve, reheat in hot oven for 10 minutes.

STEP 4: While anchovies are frying, hard-cook 1 or 2 eggs. Cool. Shell them. Slice thin. Wash romaine, cut into serving pieces. Store in refrigerator. Wash tomatoes. Salad will be put together shortly before people are expected.

STEP 5: Frozen spinach will be the easiest to serve, especially if you are having 6 people. Two packages will be needed. Cook according to directions on package.

STEP 6: Set table. Put coffee and water in pot. Get dressed. Relax.

STEP 7: Turn on oven about the time people are due, with control set at 400°F. When the first guests arrive, slip the French Fried Anchovies in the oven to reheat, and, at the same time, put the casserole in the oven. Remove the anchovies after 10 or 15 minutes. While people are enjoying these tasty morsels, cook the spinach, and finish putting the salad together, adding the dressing. Drain and chop the spinach carefully, adding plenty of butter, and a few drops of lemon juice. Then, when the casserole has a golden crust on it, you can set everything on the buffet and let your guests come have it.

MENU

Cocktail Appetizers
Spaghetti with Black Olive and Caper Sauce
Mixed Green Salad
Blackberry Jam Layer Cake   Coffee

FOR EIGHT

For this particular spaghetti sauce, you must have the imported black olives cured in brine. It's the sharp flavor of these olives-out-of-a-barrel which gives the sauce its character. You should also have Chianti, or some other dry wine, to go with this meal. As for bread, get crusty French or Italian bread, and use it to sop up the last traces of this delicious sauce.

STEP 1: Make the spaghetti sauce, using fresh tomatoes if they are in season, and therefore plentiful and cheap. Otherwise, canned tomatoes will do. Allow plenty of time for simmering the sauce, hours, if possible.

BLACK OLIVE AND	3 cloves garlic, minced
CAPER SAUCE	1 cup minced onion
	1 green pepper, minced
	6 slices bacon, chopped, or
	¼ cup olive oil
	¾ teaspoon salt
	1 teaspoon sugar
	¼ cup sherry
	6 large tomatoes, or
	3 cups canned tomatoes
	1 6-ounce can tomato paste
	1 teaspoon oregano
	½ teaspoon basil
	1 cup pitted black olives
	2 tablespoons capers

First chop the bacon into ½-inch squares. Put in large skillet and brown slightly, but do *not* cook until crisp. Add minced onion, garlic, and green pepper. Cook until soft but not brown. Add salt, tomatoes, sugar, basil, and oregano. If using fresh tomatoes, simmer at least 2 hours. The canned tomatoes do not need quite so much time. Cover. Keep at lowest heat. Add water as needed. (Vague as this sounds, one can't be any more specific because evaporation of water varies according to the kind of cooking utensil, the intensity of the heat, and other factors often beyond control.) Keep the sauce the consistency of thin cream. Halfway through, add sherry. When sauce has cooked down to the right consistency to serve with spaghetti, add the pitted, chopped black olives and the capers. Plan to simmer sauce for at least 15 minutes again just before serving.

This sauce may be prepared a day, or more, ahead of time. It improves with age.

STEP 2: Prepare the dessert. To make BLACKBERRY JAM LAYER CAKE use either a prepared mix or any standard recipe for white cake. Bake it in two layers. Spread ½ cup blackberry jam between the layers. Ice top and sides either with Lemon Icing, or

CREAM CHEESE FROSTING   1 3-ounce package cream cheese
½ teaspoon vanilla
1 cup confectioners' sugar

Whip cream cheese, softened at room temperature, with a wooden spoon. Gradually beat in the sugar, adding a little at a time. Flavor with vanilla, or not, as you like. A little grated lemon rind, about ½ teaspoon, and about one teaspoon of lemon juice may be used for flavoring instead.

STEP 3: Prepare cocktail appetizers. Copy ideas from antipasto, serving some of the same things that traditionally appear on an antipasto platter, but in a form that can be eaten with the fingers. For example, salami: spread with chive cheese, roll up, and secure with toothpicks. Anchovies: spread melba toast rounds with Radish Butter and place a curled anchovy on the top. Celery: stuff it with a processed cheese or shrimp paste. Garlic Olives and Curried Tuna Fish canapés follow the same idea.

STEP 4: Wash salad greens. Cut into serving pieces. Place in garlic-rubbed salad bowl, in refrigerator. Mix your dressing in advance, or at the table, as you prefer.

STEP 5: After people have come and the appetizers are beginning to disappear, start water boiling for the spaghetti. A pound of spaghetti should be enough for 8 people, a pound and a half will certainly be ample. Don't skimp on the spaghetti, whatever you do. It can always be used next day in a casserole—or in an omelet.

RICE
is nice at any hour

MENU

Cocktail Appetizers
Jambalaya   Mixed Green Salad
Cherry Pie   Coffee

FOR SIX

Buffet supper? This is a natural! Double the quantity for 12, triple for 18. You don't have to worry about exact proportions in making a Jambalaya. Just before serving, taste to make sure it's good, has the proper amount of salt, etc.

STEP 1: Prepare the dessert. Use any standard recipe for baking CHERRY PIE. To keep the bottom crust from getting soggy, sift a little sugar and a little flour over the crust before you add the fruit. Then place crust in oven 2 or 3 minutes before adding fruit. And into the fruit, along with the sugar, mix 1 tablespoon tapioca. This gives the juice a jelly-like consistency. Roll out the rest of the pastry, cut in long strips, and form a latticework top. It's pretty to see the red fruit peeping through.

STEP 2: Wash the salad greens, cut into serving pieces. Store in vegetable freshener or plastic bag in refrigerator. The Jambalaya is so much of a mixture, it's a good idea to keep the salad plain, though you might crumble up a bit of Roquefort or other blue cheese in the dressing.

STEP 3: Prepare cocktail appetizers. You might offer Smoked Salmon Canapés, Meat Balls Tartare, and Stuffed Radishes.

SMOKED SALMON
CANAPÉS

Cut thin-sliced dark pumpernickel bread into 1½-inch squares. Spread softened cream cheese on the bread. On the cheese place a square of smoked salmon, cut to size. Wrap these carefully in aluminum foil and keep in the refrigerator until ready to serve.

STEP 4: Get the Jambalaya ready to cook.

JAMBALAYA

1 chicken (2 or 3 pounds)
½ cup chopped ham
(or sliced ham)
6 small sausages
2 tablespoons fat
1 cup rice
⅔ cup chopped onion
2 garlic cloves, minced
1 cup canned tomatoes
2 cups water
½ teaspoon salt
¼ teaspoon marjoram
¼ teaspoon thyme
1 bay leaf

The ham may come from a leftover roast. Or, if you have no ham on hand, parboil a smoked picnic butt, and cut off a few slices. The rest of the smoked butt may be used for sandwiches, with macaroni, or in one of a half dozen ways.

In a large skillet, the largest you have, melt the fat and brown the chicken, which has been cut into 10 pieces (2 wings, 2 legs, 2 thighs, 2 breasts, 2 backs). When the chicken is nicely golden on both sides, remove it. Now add the chopped onion and garlic. Cook until soft but not browned. Then add the uncooked rice, and stir until every grain is well coated with fat. Add the tomatoes, water, salt, herbs, and the ham, and replace the chicken in the skillet, on top of the rice. (You may find it necessary to use the skillet only for browning, then transfer everything to a large casserole or kettle which can be used for top-of-the-stove simmering.) Cover. Set aside until after everyone has arrived.

Then, turn the heat on under the pot for 30 minutes before dinner is to be served. Brown the sausages separately while the Jambalaya simmers, and add as garnish.

Any number of variations are possible with this old Creole dish. Shrimp is often added. Green peppers are good with it too. Bacon may be substituted for ham, in which case, brown the bacon along with the onion. Crab or lobster may also be added.

(The Jambalaya may be baked in the oven instead of cooked on top of the stove, if that seems easier. Allow 40 minutes to bake, at 375°F., in a covered casserole.)

MENU

Cocktail Appetizers
Paella Valenciana   Asparagus Salad
Chocolate Mint Cake   Coffee

FOR EIGHT

Save this for people you really want to impress. The Paella is something like the better known Spanish dish, Arroz con Pollo [Rice with Chicken], but with shellfish added to make it that much more special.

STEP 1: Prepare the dessert. To make CHOCOLATE MINT CAKE use either a prepared cake mix or any standard recipe for chocolate cake, baking it in a square or oblong pan. After it has been removed from the oven, turn out onto a cookie sheet or a larger pan. Spread chocolate mint wafers over the top from edge to edge. Slip back into the still warm oven and leave until the wafers have all melted (about 4 minutes). This is the frosting. With a knife, swirl the melted chocolate around the top and sides of the cake while still soft and warm. This gives a marbelized effect, and it's delicious to eat.

STEP 2: Use canned asparagus for the ASPARAGUS SALAD, or precook fresh or frozen asparagus. Allow 3 spears per person. Serve cold on shredded head lettuce with French dressing. The lettuce can be washed and shredded ahead of time, and kept in a plastic bag. Have asparagus ready on a platter, mix French dressing, so that at dinnertime you can put the three together quickly on individual salad plates.

STEP 3: Arrange cocktail appetizers in bowls. The Paella will require considerable last-minute attention, so get ready-to-serve appetizers from the grocery or delicatessen, like black olives, potato chips, pretzels, popcorn, etc.

STEP 4: About an hour before guests are due, prepare first part of

PAELLA VALENCIANA

1 or 2 young broilers, 2½ to 3 pounds each
3 lobster tails
1 dozen mussels
½ pound large shrimp
1 pound peas (or 1 box frozen peas)
¼ cup pimiento, cut in strips
2 cups chicken broth
1 bouillon cube
¼ cup sherry
2 cloves garlic, minced
½ bay leaf
¼ cup olive oil
¼ cup chopped onion
1 cup canned tomatoes

Have the lobster tails cracked in 3 parts. Cut the chicken into 8 pieces. (One chicken will be enough, if it is as large as 3 pounds. If broilers are very small, better have 2.) Take out the necks, wing tips, the giblets, and the bonier section of back and use for making broth or stock. Cover these with water, add about ½ teaspoon of salt, celery leaves, and half an onion. Simmer covered for 30 to 40 minutes. Strain to make the 2 cups of chicken broth called for, adding water to make the full 2 cups if necessary.

Clean the mussels by rinsing in several waters, then vigorously brushing with a stiff brush to get out all sand. This is quite a job, and explains why mussels have not become a very popular American dish. Throw away any mussels which are open the slightest bit.

Remove shells from raw shrimp. Cut out black vein running down the back. (Or you may use frozen shrimp.)

Shell the peas (unless you are using frozen peas). Chop the garlic and onion. Cut pimiento in strips.

Now heat the olive oil in a large skillet, or an earthenware casserole. It should be an attractive utensil, for you are supposed to serve the Paella from the dish in which it is cooked. Brown the chicken in oil. Remove. Then add garlic, onion, and pimiento. Stir until golden in color. Now add uncooked rice. Stir this until all grains are well coated with oil. Add tomatoes, chicken broth, bouillon cube, peas, bay leaf, and sherry. Stir. Arrange chicken, shrimp, and lobster over the top. Stick mussels around the rice, upright, to form a pattern. Cover.

The Paella is now ready to cook, but don't turn heat on under it until after everyone has arrived.

STEP 5: Set table. Put water and coffee in pot. Get dressed.

STEP 6: After the first guests have arrived, turn the heat on under the Paella. Keep an eye on the time, for it should cook just 30 minutes. During the last 5 minutes, put the salad together. Call everyone to the table. Light the candles. Then bring in the heavy casserole with its little black mussels, its round pink shrimp, its golden chicken, and the red, red lobster tails winking out from the rice.

(A pinch of saffron is usually added to Paella, which makes the rice yellow, but I personally can't be persuaded that it alters the taste greatly, so I leave it out.)

Careful the way you handle that Paella. The casserole is *heavy*.

MENU

Cocktail Appetizers
Risotto with Sausage   *Broccoli with Hollandaise*
Tomato and Lettuce Salad
Oranges with Toasted Almonds   *Coffee*

FOR FOUR

Risotto is the same to Italians as pilaf to Greeks, Turks, and

Armenians. As a matter of fact, the two names are virtually synonymous. In this version of Risotto, tomato paste is stirred into the rice as it cooks, and Italian sausage garnishes it. Risotto can also be served with chicken, liver, or fillets of fish.

STEP 1: Prepare cocktail appetizers. A very tasty beginner for this meal would be

GRILLED CHEESE CANAPÉS	¼ cup grated American cheese
	¼ teaspoon salt
	4 tablespoons butter
	¼ teaspoon hot cayenne pepper

Let butter get very soft, then mix with remaining ingredients, forming a paste. Spread on melba toast rounds. *Just before serving,* slip under the broiler, letting the cheese become crisp and bubbly. Serve hot.

STEP 2: Prepare the dessert, ORANGES WITH TOASTED ALMONDS. Cut up oranges. Arrange in dessert dishes. Add 1 tablespoon sugar to each dish. Have a bowl of chopped, toasted almonds ready to sprinkle over the oranges just before taking them to the table.

STEP 3: Make Hollandaise Sauce for the broccoli. Cut broccoli into small pieces. Place in saucepan.

STEP 4: Wash lettuce. Cut into serving pieces. Store in refrigerator. Within the last hour before dinner, wash and quarter tomatoes, combine with lettuce in garlic-rubbed salad bowl.

STEP 5: Set table. Put water and coffee in pot.

STEP 6: Get everything ready for making the Risotto—the onions chopped, the sausage cut into serving pieces, the cheese grated, but do not actually start cooking it until after everyone has arrived.

RISOTTO WITH SAUSAGE	4 tablespoons butter or olive oil
	2 tablespoons minced onion
	1 cup rice
	1 pound Italian sausage
	¼ cup tomato paste
	3 cups water or stock
	½ cup grated Parmesan cheese
	½ teaspoon salt

Melt butter or oil in a heavy saucepan. Add the chopped onion, then the rice. Stir until every grain of rice is coated with fat. Then slowly add the water or stock, a little at a time. (Canned clear chicken soup can be used, or 3 bouillon cubes dissolved in the water.) When all water, or stock, has been added, stir in the tomato paste. Place sausage, cut into serving pieces, over the top of the rice. Simmer, covered, about 20 minutes. If rice has not yet absorbed all the liquid, uncover and cook another 5 minutes.

Meantime, cook broccoli in salted water until barely tender. Warm Hollandaise by placing over hot (not boiling) water. When rice is ready, add grated cheese, stirring it through the mixture. Arrange in a serving dish garnished with sprigs of water cress.

Put salad together. Mix dressing at table.

MENU

Cocktail Appetizers
Rice with Chicken Livers and Avocado
Lima Beans   Corn on Cob
Olive and Egg Salad
Cherry Sundae   Coffee

FOR SIX

A quick meal to put together after the theater or a day at the beach, or some other such outing. Everything waits in the refrigerator to be put together in a matter of minutes after you return home.

STEP 1: For the dessert, CHERRY SUNDAE, buy vanilla ice cream and keep in freezing compartment of refrigerator. Add a tablespoonful of brandy, kirsch, Benedictine, or some other liqueur to cherry preserves. At dessert time, add this as a sauce to the ice cream.

STEP 2: Hard-cook 2 eggs. Shell. Wash lettuce, cut into serving pieces, store in plastic bag or vegetable freshener. When the time comes, you will combine ½ cup sliced pimiento-stuffed olives with the sliced cooked eggs and lettuce, dress with Russian dressing (mayonnaise to which is added 1 tablespoon tomato catsup and 1 tablespoon chopped sweet pickle).

STEP 3: Prepare cocktail appetizers. Either serve something ready to eat from the grocer or delicatessen, or fix a canapé spread the preceding day. Corned Beef Canapés or Shrimp Tarragon would be good.

STEP 4: Strip husks and silk from corn. Keep in plastic bag in refrigerator. Plan to cook 5 minutes before dinner is to be served, plunging ears of corn into water already rapidly boiling. Use frozen limas. These, too, require only brief cooking time when added to boiling water.

STEP 5: While the others are enjoying cocktails, and nibbling on the appetizers, prepare

RICE WITH CHICKEN LIVERS	1½ cups rice
AND AVOCADO	1 can concentrated tomato soup
	1 package frozen chicken livers
	1 or 2 avocados

Wash rice through several waters until water is clear. Add tomato soup and water enough to make 4 cups liquid. Cover. Cook for 20 minutes, or until rice has absorbed liquid.

Meantime, while rice cooks, grill chicken livers in 1 *tablespoon butter*, turning to brown on both sides. Dust them with salt from a shaker after removing from the skillet. Peel the avocado and slice.

STEP 6: Start heating water for both corn and limas when you start cooking the rice. Cook each 5 minutes. Put salad together.

STEP 7: Rice will probably be cooked by now. To serve, garnish rice with chicken livers and with slices of avocado.

Fill the coffeepot, and let the beverage be strong and black.

MENU

Cocktail Appetizers
Pilaf with Lamb
Green Salad with Black Olives
Lemon Meringue Tarts   Coffee

FOR SIX

You might imagine yourself within sight of the Acropolis as you enjoy this meal. It's Greek to the core.

Not quite party fare—it's simple and wholesome, not highly seasoned. Best for a quiet evening with old friends.

STEP 1: Parboil 2 lamb shanks in salted water for 1 hour, or until very tender. You will use the broth they cooked in for the Pilaf. The meat, cut from the bones, will also go into the final dish.

STEP 2: While the lamb simmers, prepare dessert. For variety, instead of lemon meringue pie, make individual Lemon Meringue Tarts. Lemon pie is in the true Greek spirit, for Greek restaurateurs, returning to the old country from America, have made it a well-known dessert in Athens. To make tarts, use 1½ cups flour for the dough. Divide dough into 6 portions for easier handling. Use inverted muffin tins, or individual tart pans. The same amount of filling as required for a 9-inch pie will fill 6 tart shells. Here is the old standard recipe for Lemon Meringue Tarts which I find always good:

LEMON MERINGUE TARTS

5 tablespoons cornstarch
2 cups water
1 cup sugar
¼ teaspoon salt
3 egg yolks
2 or 3 tablespoons butter
⅓ cup lemon juice
2 teaspoons grated lemon rind
2 tablespoons confectioners' sugar
3 egg whites

Mix together cornstarch, sugar, and salt. Slowly add water. Cook in the top of a double boiler until mixture begins to boil (or cook directly over low heat, stirring constantly). Cover, cook at low heat for 10 minutes. Beat egg yolks until thick, pour a little of cornstarch mixture over the yolks, blending thoroughly, then combine the two mixtures. Return to double boiler. Cook 2 or 3 minutes longer. Remove from heat, add butter, lemon juice, and rind. Mix well. Cool. Pour into tart shells or pie shell already baked. Beat egg whites until stiff, stir in 2 tablespoons confectioners' sugar (or granulated sugar will do). Spread over the lemon filling. Bake in a 300°F. oven 15 or 20 minutes, or until golden brown.

Shredded coconut may be spread over the meringue before it is placed in the oven, for an additional flourish.

STEP 3: Prepare cocktail appetizers. The best beginner for this meal would be Marinated Grilled Shrimp. Another typically Greek appetizer is artichoke hearts, which come ready to serve in jars, and can be speared with toothpicks to be eaten by hand.

STEP 4: Wash salad greens. Cut into serving pieces. Store in plastic bag, or place in salad bowl already rubbed with garlic. Remove seeds from black olives, add to greens. At table, mix with lemon juice, olive oil, salt and pepper.

STEP 5: Shell peas to go into Pilaf (see below).

STEP 6: Make

TOMATO SAUCE

1 6-ounce can tomato paste
1 can condensed tomato soup
¼ teaspoon oregano or thyme
1 bouillon cube
1 cup water
¼ cup sherry

Mix all ingredients together. Heat in a saucepan until bouillon cube dissolves. Put aside to serve with Pilaf.

STEP 7: Set table. Put water and coffee in pot. Relax.

STEP 8: After everyone has come, grill the cocktail shrimps. Then, while the guests enjoy cocktails and appetizers, make the Pilaf.

PILAF WITH LAMB

1½ cups rice
4 tablespoons butter
4½ cups lamb broth
Meat from 2 lamb shanks
1 pound peas, shelled

Melt butter in a heavy saucepan. Add rice and stir around until every grain seems to be well coated with butter. Add peas and lamb, and slowly add the lamb broth. Cover. After liquid has reached boiling point. turn heat to lowest point and simmer for 20 minutes, or until rice has absorbed liquid. At table, pass Tomato Sauce (you will reheat this as Pilaf cooks) to be poured over the Pilaf. Grated Parmesan cheese is sometimes served with Pilaf too, sprinkled over the top as with spaghetti.

Look to the Timeless East

So popular have curry dishes become that it's now common to see them listed on restaurant menus all across the country. Yet few of these curries would ever be recognized in India. Flour should never be used in a curry, but garlic always should be.

The recipe given below is basic, and can be used with any other meat, or with chicken. Raisins and apple are both optional additions, but oddly enough they help to thicken the curry sauce and to give it a special piquancy, so I urge their inclusion. Curry tastes better when reheated. A working girl can prepare a curry the day before-hand, then only have to reheat it a few minutes before serving on The Night. As a matter of fact, curry can even be made several days be-forehand, as long as it's kept under refrigeration. And when any is left over, store it in the freezing compartment of your refrigerator (or in the freezer, if you have one). Take it out a week or a month later, and it tastes still better.

STEP 1: Prepare

BEEF CURRY

3 pounds beef, boneless chuck
1 or 2 cloves garlic, minced
½ cup onion, chopped fine
2 tablespoons vegetable fat
1½ tablespoons curry powder
½ cup seedless raisins
1 medium apple (optional)
3½ cups water
1 green pepper, minced (optional)
½ to ¾ teaspoon salt

Cut the beef into 1-inch cubes. Melt the fat in a large skillet. Add the beef, and brown quickly on all sides. Then lower heat, add onions, garlic, green pepper, and salt. Now add the curry powder, stirring it to blend thoroughly with the meat and chopped vegetables. The quality of the curry powder is all-important. Splurge on the very best you can find. The cheaper curry powders are sharper, with a much larger proportion of tumeric, and can ruin the dish entirely. Finally add the raisins, sliced apples, and water, and cover. Simmer at least 1 hour, until meat is tender when pricked with a fork. Put aside until ready to reheat and serve.

(To serve 4 persons, simply cut the above recipe in half and taste carefully for seasoning. However, it's so good when left over, you might as well make the whole recipe, whatever the number of diners, then get it out again next week, if you do have any left.)

STEP 2: While curry simmers, arrange the condiments in bowls. You could, of course, make your own chutney if you wanted to go to that much trouble. But there are several excellent chutneys on the market. Major Grey's is the most famous. The other condiments suggested can all be purchased at the grocers. These are to be passed as garnish for the curry.

STEP 3: Prepare cocktail appetizers. Chicken Livers in Bacon would be excellent to precede this meal. Buy either the frozen chicken livers, or get them by the quarter pound from a poultry-in-parts shop, or from the supermarket.

Also good would be Shrimp Tarragon with the shrimp served whole on melba toast rounds, topped with the tarragon mayonnaise.

STEP 4: Wash salad greens. Cut into serving pieces. Store in refrigerator.

STEP 5: Wash rice through several waters until water is clear. Measure out correct amount of water and salt with rice in a saucepan. Cover. Keep on back of stove until 20 minutes before dinner is to be served.

STEP 6: For the dessert, RASPBERRIES AND PEACHES WITH COINTREAU, get frozen peaches and frozen raspberries. For 8 people, you will probably need 3 packages, so get 2 of peaches and one of raspberries. For a smaller number, get 1 package of each. Take from freezing compartment at least 2 hours before dinner is to be served, but keep on a lower shelf of the refrigerator so fruit will remain chilled. Open the packages within the last hour before guests are due, and add 2 tablespoons Cointreau if you have 2 packages of fruit, 3 tablespoons of Cointreau for 3 packages. A simple but really luscious dessert. Everyone will like it.

STEP 7: Set table, putting condiments on the table in bowls. Put coffee and water in pot. Get dressed. About the time people are due, turn on broiler so that bacon appetizers may be quickly broiled.

STEP 8: After every one has arrived, quickly brown the liver-in-bacon appetizers, then pass these and the Shrimp Tarragon. While your guests enjoy the appetizers, cook the rice, reheat the curry, and put the salad together. If the curry sauce seems to have thickened too much, add a little more liquid. The sauce should be about the consistency of a daiquiri full of shaved ice.

Come to think of it, daiquiris might be a good cocktail to serve on this occasion, especially if it's summertime and warm.

MENU

Cocktail Appetizers
Moussaka   Green Salad
Fruit Punch Cup   Coffee

FOR EIGHT

There's nothing so new, really, about one-dish meals. This Balkan dish is centuries old. Many different Balkan countries claim Moussaka as a national dish. Probably it originated in Turkey. The recipe for Moussaka that follows I learned from Greek friends.

STEP 1: Start preparing

MOUSSAKA

1 small eggplant
½ cup vegetable shortening
2 tablespoons butter
1 pound ground meat
¾ teaspoon salt
4 medium onions, sliced
3 cloves garlic, minced
½ teaspoon thyme
½ teaspoon oregano
2 eggs, separated
8 tablespoons fine bread crumbs
½ cup white wine
½ cup canned tomatoes

The skin of the eggplant is very important in the flavor of this dish, so do *not* peel it. Slice lengthwise, then cut slices into pieces easy to handle in the frying pan or skillet. Melt part of the shortening in the skillet. Place the eggplant slices in hot fat, and brown on both sides. Keep on adding fat as you need it. The skillet must not be allowed to get dry at any time. You may find more than ½ cup of shortening necessary. Pile the eggplant slices on a plate as you remove them from the skillet.

Next, prepare the meat mixture. Almost any ground meat may be used: beef, lamb, or veal, or a combination. Lamb is the meat used in Greece, because it's the most common and the cheapest meat there. Since ground beef is more readily available and cheaper here, that is what I generally use. Melt the 2 tablespoons of butter in a second

skillet. Add the onions and garlic. Stir until soft. Add the meat, ½
teaspoon salt, herbs, tomatoes, and wine. Cover. Simmer 30 minutes.
Cool. Then add the 2 unbeaten egg whites (keeping the egg yolk for
the Béchamel Sauce) and 4 tablespoons of fine bread crumbs.

Next, grease a large casserole, a 10- or 12-inch size. Lay the remaining bread crumbs over the bottom. Place a layer of eggplant on
the crumbs, then a layer of the meat mixture, another layer of eggplant, etc., until the ingredients are used up.

Then make the

BÉCHAMEL SAUCE	2 tablespoons butter
	2 tablespoons flour
	½ teaspoon salt
	1½ cups milk
	2 egg yolks
	⅛ teaspoon nutmeg

Melt the butter in the top of a double boiler. Add the flour, stirring
until smooth. Add salt and milk. When sauce has thickened and is
smooth, pour a little of the hot sauce, about 1 tablespoonful at a
time, over the beaten egg yolks in a bowl. When half the sauce has
been added to the yolks, combine the mixture in the bowl with that
in the double boiler—a reverse motion. Finally add the nutmeg.

Pour this sauce over the Moussaka, so that it covers the top.
(When the Mousska is baked, this sauce will form a soft crust, golden
on top, white underneath.)

Put the casserole aside, on the back of the stove, until 15 or 20
minutes before guests are expected. Then it is to be baked in a
moderate (350°F.) oven for a total of 1 hour.

STEP 2: Prepare dessert.

FRUIT PUNCH CUP	1 medium pineapple
	1 pint strawberries, sliced,
	or 1 package frozen strawberries
	2 or 3 oranges
	½ cup white wine
	¼ cup brandy
	½ cup sugar (about)

Dice the pineapple, after slicing and trimming carefully and cutting out hard center. Peel and cut up oranges. If fresh berries are used, go over them carefully and use only the best. Slice. Add ¼ cup sugar to the berries. (If frozen strawberries are used, drain most of the liquid, do not add sugar.) Combine the three fruits. Add the wine and the brandy, and a little more sugar. Taste. Use your own judgment as to how much sugar is needed, for fruits differ greatly in natural sweetness. Let fruits marinate in the wine and brandy in the refrigerator, all day if possible. Transfer to sherbet dishes at dessert time.

Instead of white wine and brandy, you might add sherry and rum, in the same proportions, or claret and rum, or you might use ½ cup orange juice and 3 tablespoons kirsch. Glance over your liquor supply to see what you have on hand, and experiment a little. You can combine liquors in small quantity in a shot glass to see how they go together.

STEP 3: Prepare cocktail appetizers. Black olives are a natural, especially if you can find the imported Greek olives bottled in red wine vinegar and olive oil. Cheese popcorn, and Shrimp-Avocado Canapés would go well too.

STEP 4: Wash salad greens thoroughly. Cut into serving pieces. Store in refrigerator. For the dressing, use fresh lemon juice, with oil, salt, pepper, and a little dry mustard.

STEP 5: Set table. Put coffee and water in pot. Get dressed.

STEP 6: Put the Moussaka in the oven. About the time guests are due, turn the oven on. Relax. Try a cocktail and one of your cocktail appetizers while you wait for the doorbell to ring.

MENU

Cocktail Appetizers
Chicken Marinated in Yogurt
Rice   Peas
Salad of Olives, Chicory, Romaine
Spice Cake with Banana Frosting   Coffee

FOR SIX

The idea of marinating chicken in yogurt comes from Pakistan. If you can find ginger root, a little of this chopped up and added to the yogurt makes the roast chicken even more wonderful. Ginger root can be found in Chinese groceries, so if there is a Chinatown near you, shop for some. It will keep for some time, and you will find many other uses for it.

STEP 1: Start preparing the

CHICKEN MARINATED	1 5-pound roasting chicken
IN YOGURT	½ pint yogurt
	2 tablespoons chopped ginger root
	2 small onions
	¼ cup butter (4 tablespoons)
	1 teaspoon salt

The chicken should be left whole, with an onion placed in the cavity. Prick skin of chicken all over with a fork so that the yogurt will penetrate it. Then peel the ginger root and chop very fine. Peel the second onion and chop fine. Combine ginger root, chopped onion, salt, and yogurt and pour over chicken. With the back of a spoon, vigorously rub the mixture into the skin of the chicken. Allow chicken to stand like this for at least 1 hour, several hours will be better. Start roasting it, in the same casserole or roasting pan used for the marinade, 2½ hours at least before you expect to put dinner on the table. The oven should be set at 325°F. (If you are to be away all day, pour the marinade over the chicken in the morning. Put it in the oven to marinate. Turn the oven on as soon as you get home.)

(If you can't find ginger root, simply leave it out. The chicken will still be good.)

STEP 2: Prepare dessert. Bake a spice cake either in 2 layers, or in a square cake pan, using a prepared mix or a standard recipe. Top it with the following

BANANA FROSTING	½ cup mashed banana
	(1 or 2 bananas)
	¼ cup butter, softened
	½ teaspoon lemon juice
	3½ cups sifted confectioners' sugar

To mash the banana, cut into slices, then press down with a rotary beater, and beat until a smooth pulp is formed. Measure out to exactly ½ cup. Beat butter until creamy in a mixing bowl. Add sugar and mashed banana alternately to the butter, beating after each addition. Add the lemon juice last, beating thoroughly after it is added.

(This is enough, as is, for the top and sides of a square 8 x 8-inch cake. If you bake the cake in 2 layers, add some of the frosting to the bottom layer before all the sugar has been added, while it is still a little on the fluid side. This helps to make it go farther, to make enough for the entire frosting job.)

STEP 3: Prepare cocktail appetizers. Pistachio nuts, Water Cress Canapés, and

PIMIENTO ANCHOVY CANAPÉS

Spread melba toast rounds with butter. Cut pieces of pimiento to fit the toast rounds. Top with a curled fillet of anchovy. These canapés may be made hours beforehand and kept in the refrigerator until time to serve. They improve with waiting.

STEP 4: Wash salad greens, cut into serving pieces, store in refrigerator. Place salad in garlic-rubbed bowl, with olives, during the last hour before guests are expected.

STEP 5: Wash rice, measure out with salt and water in saucepan. Cover. Leave on back of stove until 20 minutes before dinner is to be served.

STEP 6: Shell peas. Place on back of stove. (Or use frozen peas, following directions on package, or canned peas.)

STEP 7: Two hours before guests are expected, turn on oven and put chicken in to roast. Then set table, put coffee and water in pot, get dressed, and read a book or listen to the radio.

STEP 8: After everyone has arrived and appetizers are being enjoyed, start rice and peas cooking, put salad together. Chicken should be tender now, and luscious. The yogurt will have been completely absorbed, and you will find the skin crisp and brown but with a special flavor. Remove chicken from casserole or roaster, and add ½ to ¾ cup water, stirring up all the gelatinous bits on the bottom of the pan as the water heats to boiling. (If an earthenware casserole was used to roast the chicken, transfer the sauce to a pan in which water can be heated to boiling.) Boil until liquid is reduced to half. Add salt to taste, a scanty ½ teaspoon will be about right. Pour this sauce into a gravy boat, to be poured over rice. Serve the chicken on a platter, to be carved at table.

MENU

Cocktail Appetizers
Shrimp Bouillon
Ginger Beef
Rice   Chinese Cabbage or Chard
Preserved Kumquats on Ice Cream   Tea or Coffee

FOR FOUR

Ordinarily, serving soup as a first course seems more bother than it's worth in a servantless ménage. However, this Chinese soup is very easy to prepare, and so delicious it is worth the bother. As for the Ginger Beef, if you located some of that ginger root mentioned in the previous menu, you'll be all set to make this easy yet very unusual Chinese beef dish.

STEP 1: Prepare the marinade for

GINGER BEEF
1 cup soy sauce
½ cup honey
3 cloves garlic, minced
1½ pounds round steak, sliced
    paper-thin
3 tablespoons minced ginger root
3 tablespoons oil or fat

Ask the butcher to slice the top round through his machine just as if it were boiled ham or salami. Then, when you get the meat at home, cut the paper-thin slices into narrow fingers 2 or 3 inches in length. Marinate the meat in the soy sauce, honey, and minced garlic. (No salt is needed, for the soy sauce provides enough.) Meantime, chop

164

the ginger root as fine as possible, then put aside in a bowl.

Only 3 to 5 minutes' cooking time is required for this dish. You will wait until *only a few minutes before dinner is to be served,* then heat the oil or vegetable fat in a large skillet, add the ginger root, and then lift the meat from its marinade, adding a little at a time, to the hot fat. When all has been added, bring the liquid to a boil, turn the fire low, and cook just 3 minutes. Turn off heat, cover, to keep it warm during the soup course.

STEP 2: Prepare cocktail appetizers. Lobster Salad Canapés and Stuffed Radishes would both be appropriate.

STEP 3: Cut either Chinese Cabbage or Swiss chard into 1-inch pieces. Precook in ½ cup water and ¼ teaspoon salt for 3 minutes. Drain. Put aside. The Chinese way is to marinate a little lean pork, fine strips of it cut from the loin, and then to cook the pork with the cabbage or chard. If you want to try this, cut the meat from 1 loin pork chop, carefully discarding every bit of fat. Then marinate these strips of pork in:

> 1 teaspoon sugar
> 1 tablespoon soy sauce
> 1½ tablespoons flour
> 1½ tablespoons oil

After the meat has been standing in this sauce for an hour or longer, heat 2 tablespoons of oil in a skillet, add the pork to this, carefully draining first. Cook over high heat, tossing lightly with a fork, until all the pork is lightly browned. Put this in another bowl.

Shortly before the meal is to be served, either just before or just after you cook the Ginger Beef, heat another 2 tablespoons of oil in a skillet, add the partially cooked cabbage or chard and cover, letting it cook 2 minutes, or until barely tender. Then add the pork, and cook another 2 minutes, until the pork is heated through.

(If you do not care to add the pork, finish cooking the vegetable at the last minute simply by placing in a skillet with 2 tablespoons of oil, cover tightly, and cook over high heat until barely tender.)

STEP 4: Wash the rice thoroughly, through several waters, stirring with your fingers or a spoon, until the water is clear. Then measure with water and salt in a saucepan and leave on the back of the stove until 20 minutes before the meal is to be served.

STEP 5: Shell the raw shrimps for

SHRIMP BOUILLON   ¼ pound fresh shrimp
                                 1 can concentrated beef bouillon

Shell and de-vein the shrimp. Put aside in a bowl. You will not cook the shrimp until *just before the meal is to be served.* Then you will pour the canned bouillon in a saucepan, add an equal amount of water, and bring this to a boil. Then add the shrimp and simmer until the shrimp have become pink. The bouillon will take on the shrimp flavor.

STEP 6: For the dessert, KUMQUATS ON ICE CREAM, buy a jar of preserved kumquats, and a pint of vanilla ice cream. Keep the ice cream in the freezing compartment of your refrigerator until the dessert course is due. Then remove, and serve in dessert dishes with the kumquats and their sirup as garnish.

STEP 7: Set table. Get out the teapot, or the coffeepot, or both. Get dressed. Relax.

STEP 8: After your guests have arrived, as they enjoy the appetizers, put this Chinese meal together. No one dish takes long to cook, so while the preparations are complicated, the actual cooking time will be brief.

First, start the rice. Then, the Ginger Beef. After you have started the Ginger Beef, cook the cabbage or chard. Finally, heat the bouillon and add the fresh shrimp. By the time the rice is cooked, all your other dishes should be ready. Keep the dishes for the main course covered so that they will stay warm while you have the soup course.

As the soup is being sipped, boil water for tea. If you are going to serve tea, take the trouble to brew it properly. This means, first, heat the teapot thoroughly with boiling water. Discard the water, then add tea leaves to the heated pot, allowing ½ teaspoon per cup. Over the tea leaves, pour water that has been boiling full steam for a good 3 minutes. Then let it brew for another 5 minutes. You'll have tea that *is* tea, and not the usual faintly colored tasteless amber water.

MENU

Cocktail Appetizers
Shashlyk
Rice and Peas (Pilaf)
Green Salad
Ice Cream Tarts   Coffee

FOR SIX

Shashlyk is supposed to be made with lamb, cut either from the loin or the leg. However, it can also be made with beef, and be just as good, whatever may be said about authenticity. What difference, if any, there is between shashlyk and shish kebab I've never been able to discover, except that one is Russian, the other the Persian or Armenian name.

This is a fine choice for an outdoor grill. It's fun to turn the spit beside an open barbecue pit, watching the meat brown and smelling the succulent fragrance that wafts up from the fire.

STEP 1: Marinate the meat for the

SHASHLYK

3 pounds top round of beef, or
   3 pounds lamb from loin or leg
½ cup wine vinegar
½ cup oil
2 or 3 garlic cloves, minced
1 teaspoon salt
½ teaspoon basil
½ teaspoon marjoram
½ teaspoon thyme
2 medium onions, sliced

Have the meat cut in 2-inch squares. Combine the vinegar, oil, salt and herbs, and the garlic. Pour this over the meat, and marinate for several hours.

To cook, spear the meat on long skewers, with a slice of onion slipped between chunks of meat every now and then. If you do not have skewers long enough, you could in an emergency use wire coat hangers cut to size. (Though if you like this dish, it would be worth while to buy skewers of the proper length.) Have the meat ready to cook, but do not put it over the fire (or under the broiler) until the cocktails are going round. This is generally a process that people like to watch. It whets the appetite to see as well as smell the meat browning.

STEP 2: Prepare the dessert. To make ICE CREAM TARTS, bake individual tart shells, one for each person. (Or you could buy patty shells from the bakery if you haven't time to make your own tart shells.) Into each tart shell, place a tablespoonful of fruit preserves. Fill the shells with ice cream. Vanilla goes with anything, but you might have banana ice cream over peach preserves. Or, try butter pecan over sliced banana, or chocolate ice cream with toasted coconut. Or dream up some other combination of your own.

STEP 3: For the pilaf, wash the rice through several waters, until water is clear. Measure out with salt and water in a saucepan. Shell 1½ pounds of peas. Place the shelled peas over the rice, in the same saucepan. Add about a tablespoon of butter. Cover. Twenty minutes before the meal is to be served, cook the rice and peas together. Tomato Sauce may be passed to be poured over the pilaf.

A few leaves of mint, either fresh or dried, are sometimes added to the pilaf too, during the cooking.

STEP 4: Wash the salad greens. Cut into serving pieces. Store in the refrigerator. Serve with a dressing of fresh lemon juice, olive oil, mustard, and salt.

STEP 5: Prepare cocktail appetizers. Red caviar and sour cream would be appropriate. Serve in two bowls, surrounded by crackers, so that they can be spread as needed. If you feel you need something more, you might have Egg and Olive Canapés. And, of course, crunchy things like pretzels, popcorn, or potato chips always help to fill the gap of time and appetite until dinner is served.

STEP 6: Set table. Put coffee and water in pot. Get yourself dressed. Relax.

STEP 7: While appetizers are being enjoyed, start cooking the pilaf. Add dressing to the salad. If you plan to serve Tomato Sauce with the pilaf, heat that now. Put the meat on the fire the very last thing, so people can watch. Cooking is fun, so you might as well make it part of the party.

MENU

Cocktail Appetizers
Turkish Eggplant and Lamb
Rice   Green Salad
Cottage Cheese Horns   Coffee

FOR EIGHT

The Bosporus is a beautiful sight at sunset. The water separating Europe from Asia burns like flame as the sun drops down, and the arid hills on either side glow with a copperish sheen. In the background you hear the mournful, monotonous wailing of Turkish singers that goes on day and night, without end.

And this is the kind of meal you would dine on, were you sitting at an outdoor restaurant in Istanbul, as the sun set. You should have a sirupy-sweet pastry for dessert, and you should have thick, sweet Turkish coffee in demitasse cups to finish off the meal. But the Turkish pastries are too much on the sticky-sweet side for American tastes, and Turkish coffee is so thick one has only about a teaspoonful of actual liquid to drink. So Americanize that part of the meal. Pick out your favorite pastry from the bakery—or make your own, if you prefer. Have regular American coffee, too, brewed in your favorite way.

STEP 1: Start cooking the

TURKISH EGGPLANT	3 or 4 pounds lamb, shanks or shoulder
AND LAMB	2 medium onions
	¾ cup olive oil
	1 medium or 2 small eggplants
	2 or 3 cloves garlic
	¾ teaspoon thyme
	¾ teaspoon salt
	1 6-ounce can tomato paste
	1 cup water

Have the meat cut into serving portions, with the bone cracked. The larger the proportion of bone the more poundage will be required. Judge for yourself how much to buy. To cook, you will need a large heavy kettle—a pressure cooker would be fine. First heat the oil (you may use vegetable fat if you prefer, but the olive oil flavor is especially good with eggplant). When the oil is hot, add the eggplant, which has been sliced lengthwise. Get 2 very small eggplants, if you can, because the skin is the most delicious part. When the eggplant is lightly browned, remove and add the onion and garlic, both minced fine. Let these get soft, but not brown, then remove and add the lamb. Sear it well. Then replace eggplant, onion, and garlic. Add salt, thyme, tomato paste, and water. Cover. Simmer gently for 2 hours. (Or cook under steam in the pressure cooker, following directions for lamb stew.) Cool. Let fat harden, then skim off lamb fat. You will reheat to serve.

STEP 2: Prepare dessert. This is not a Turkish dessert, in fact it actually is Viennese, but that makes no difference. It's good.

COTTAGE CHEESE HORNS
½ cup cottage cheese
½ cup vegetable fat
1 cup flour
1 egg yolk
1 teaspoon sugar
⅛ teaspoon salt
Jam or preserves

Cottage cheese should be the smooth kind. Mash it down and press through a sieve to get out all the lumps. Sift flour with sugar and salt. Cut in fat. Stir in egg yolk and cottage cheese. With your fingers, knead to make a dough. Wrap with aluminum foil or waxed paper and place in freezing compartment of refrigerator for at least 1 hour. Then divide into 8 portions, and roll each out on a well-floured board, forming 4-inch squares. Put 1 scant teaspoon of fruit preserves (damson plum, blackberry, raspberry, or currant jelly are best) in the center of each. Roll over and shape like a horn with the fingers. (The jam will run out the opening of the horn unless you are careful to keep it well down in the center of the dough.) If you have a pastry brush, spread a little slightly beaten egg white over each horn to make it shiny. Or a little cream would serve the same purpose.

Bake in a 400°F. oven for 25 to 30 minutes. Strew with confectioners' sugar while still warm.

(You may do the same thing with regular pastry, forgetting the cottage cheese.)

STEP 3: As cocktail appetizers, I suggest black olives, goat cheese,

and pistachio nuts. Imported goat cheese comes from several countries: Norway, Switzerland, and Greece. But if you don't find goat
cheese in the markets, serve chive cheese as a dunk for potato chips
or pretzels.

STEP 4: Wash the rice briskly until the water is clear. Add to saucepan
with correct anount of salt and water. Cover. Start cooking just 20
minutes before dinner is to be served.

STEP 5: Wash the salad greens, cut into serving portions, store in the
refrigerator. Mix with dressing at table.

STEP 6: Set table. Put coffee and water in pot. Get dressed. Relax.

STEP 7: As the cocktails are being enjoyed, reheat the Eggplant and
Lamb, and cook the rice. But don't be in a hurry to go to the table.
The dinner will wait.

MENU

Butterfly Shrimp (Cocktail Appetizer)
Chinese Steak and Green Peppers
Rice   Chinese Noodles
Mixed Salad
Apricot Pistachio Mousse   Tea or Coffee

FOR FOUR

STEP 1: Prepare the dessert. Apricot Pistachio Mousse has nothing to
do with Chinese cuisine, but it is delicate enough in flavor to be
appropriate for this meal.

APRICOT PISTACHIO   1 small can apricots
MOUSSE   ½ cup heavy cream
      1 egg white
      2 tablespoons sugar
      Few grains salt
      ¼ teaspoon almond extract
      1 tablespoon finely chopped
          pistachio nuts

You should have about ¾ to 1 cup apricot pulp, made by mashing the whole peeled apricots through a sieve. (Discard the juice.) Add the sugar, salt, vanilla, and the nuts. Beat the cream until thick. In another bowl, beat the egg white until very stiff. Fold the apricot mixture into the whipped cream, then gently fold this into the stiff egg white. Fill paper muffin cups. Place the cups close together in a refrigerator tray. Freeze at least 4 hours.

STEP 2: Butterfly Shrimp, which you would order as a main dish in a Chinese restaurant, may be served as appetizers with your cocktails. You will shell and de-vein the raw shrimp in advance, and have the batter, the deep fat, and the sauce ready, but don't fry the shrimp until after people have come, because cooking time is only 5 to 7 minutes, and the flavor will be far better if the shrimp are freshly cooked.

BUTTERFLY SHRIMP	½ pound shrimp
	½ cup pancake mix
	1 egg
	½ cup milk
SAUCE	2 teaspoons dry mustard
	1½ teaspoons vinegar
	1 teaspoon sugar
	½ teaspoon soy sauce

Have the shrimp ready in one bowl. In another bowl, have the batter mixed. (Instead of pancake mix, you may make the batter with ½ cup flour, ½ teaspoon baking powder, and ¼ teaspoon salt, with the egg and milk.) Beat the egg first, then shake in the pancake mix or your own flour mixture, and finally add the milk.

In a third bowl, mix the sauce of mustard, sugar, vinegar, and soy sauce.

Have a deep heavy saucepan ready, with the fat or oil in it. After the doorbell rings, turn on the heat under the fat. After the first cocktails have been poured, dip the raw shrimp in the batter, then fry in the sizzling-hot fat. To serve, put out small individual bowls containing the mustard sauce, so that each person can dunk the fried shrimp in his own little sauce bowl. Put a pile of paper cocktail napkins on the coffee table, for the shrimp should be eaten with the fingers.

STEP 3: Prepare the ingredients for the Steak and Green Peppers, though this will not be cooked until the last minute.

CHINESE STEAK AND
GREEN PEPPERS

1 pound round steak
1 cup minced onion
2 green peppers, cut in 1-inch squares
4 tablespoons vegetable fat or oil
6 tablespoons soy sauce
½ tablespoon cornstarch
1 cup water

Cut the meat into thin slivers. Marinate in 2 tablespoons soy sauce. Heat the fat or oil in a skillet. Add the onions. Cook until soft. Lift onions from the fat with a perforated spoon and put aside in a bowl. Add the green peppers to the fat. Cook about 2 minutes. Lift from fat and put aside in another bowl. *Later, about 10 minutes before dinner is to be served,* you will lift the meat from its marinade and brown it in the fat. It may be necessary to add more fat or oil to the skillet, depending on how much the vegetables have absorbed. Cook the meat over high heat, quickly, searing it. Then add the partially cooked vegetables, and cook another 2 or 3 minutes with the remaining soy sauce. Serve while still crisp over rice, with the crisp Chinese noodles as a garnish.

STEP 4: Wash rice through several waters, until the water is clear. Measure in a saucepan with salt and water. Cover. Leave on back of stove until 20 minutes before dinner is to be served.

STEP 5: Prepare the salad. Mixed vegetables, such as cooked limas, cooked leftover Frenched green beans, minced celery, sliced radishes, or leftover broccoli flowerlets, are marinated in French dressing. Mix with head lettuce just before guests are due.

STEP 6: Set table. Get out both teapot and coffeepot. Get dressed. And relax—you are probably a little weary by this time. Try out one of your cocktails.

STEP 7: With the arrival of the first guest, turn on the heat under the fat for the shrimp. Fry the shrimp as soon as the fat is hot enough. Take these Butterfly Shrimp to the living room, and sit with your guests to enjoy them. But before all the shrimp have been consumed, excuse yourself and start the rice cooking. Finish cooking the Steak and Green Peppers. Boil water for the tea.

Kidneys for a Fast Dish

MENU

Cocktail Appetizers
Kidneys with Mustard Sauce
Rice   Asparagus
Mixed Salad
Oranges and Dates with Grand Marnier
Coffee

FOR SIX

It's too bad kidneys are so little appreciated in this country. When properly prepared they are superb, worthy of the most discriminating palate. The greatest mistake is in cooking them too long. They become tough, and the taste becomes strong. When cooked no more than 5 minutes, they remain tender and delicate in flavor, and form the basis for marvelous sauces.

STEP 1: Prepare the dessert. For ORANGES AND DATES WITH GRAND MARNIER, peel 6 oranges and cut into small segments. Mince ½ cup dates. Combine with the oranges. Add ¼ cup sugar and 2 tablespoons Grand Marnier. Put aside, but *not* in the refrigerator. Let the fruit marinate in the liqueur until time to serve. (If you don't have any Grand Marnier, you might use brandy, Drambuie, or Cointreau.)

STEP 2: Prepare cocktail appetizers. Salmon Caper Canapés, or grilled Miniature Meat Balls, or Stuffed Radishes would all be appropriate. If you decide to have the meat balls, keep them under refrigeration until the guests have arrived, then slip under the broiler. Your guests can enjoy the other appetizers while the meat balls brown.

STEP 3: Wash the rice, measure with salt and water in a saucepan. Cover. Place on back of stove. Cook 20 minutes before dinner is to be served.

STEP 4: Scrub asparagus thoroughly with a sharp-bristled brush to get out all grit. Cut off tough portions of stalks. The best way to determine this is to take the two ends of the asparagus between your fingers and bend them. The stalk will crack at the place where the toughness starts. Lay the spears flat in a skillet, or upright in the top of a double boiler. Use only ½ cup water. Allow 5 to 10 minutes' cooking time, depending on thickness and age of spears. Cook just before serving dinner, until asparagus is barely tender. Add a generous amount of butter, a few drops of lemon juice.

(When fresh asparagus is not in season, the frozen asparagus is an excellent substitute.)

STEP 5: Wash salad greens. Cut into serving portions. Store in refrigerator. Add to the salad any bits of leftover vegetables you may have, cutting each into small pieces. Mix vegetables (but not salad greens) with French dressing, to marinate. Add greens just before taking salad to table.

(All the above can be prepared as much as 24 hours in advance, if that suits you. The meal can then be put together in a total of 20 minutes, the amount of time needed for cooking the rice. In this case, water and salt would not be added to the rice until just before it is to be cooked, but all the other steps are the same.)

STEP 6. Prepare kidneys for cooking, but *do not cook until just before dinner is to be served.*

KIDNEYS WITH MUSTARD SAUCE	12 lamb kidneys, or 2 veal kidneys 1 teaspoon prepared mustard ½ teaspoon salt ⅓ cup dry red wine 2 tablespoons butter

Melt butter in a skillet. When hot, add the sliced kidneys, turning with a fork or spatula until they are thoroughly browned. Add mustard and salt. Blend thoroughly. Add the wine. Cover. Simmer 4 or 5 minutes. Serve at once.

STEP 7: Set table. Put coffee and water in pot. Get dressed.

STEP 8: After everyone has come, put Miniature Meat Balls under the broiler. After the second round of drinks has been served, start the rice cooking, then the asparagus, and finally cook the kidneys. Put salad together during the 5 minutes the kidneys are simmering.

A chilled white wine, Chablis preferably, would be excellent with this French meal.

MENU

Cocktail Appetizers
Kidneys au Fine Champagne
Rice   Peas
Tomatoes Tarragon
Peach Bread Pudding   Coffee

FOR FOUR

STEP 1: Prepare the dessert.

PEACH BREAD PUDDING

1 cup stale bread crumbs,
white or cracked wheat
2 cups milk, heated
2 eggs, beaten together
3 medium peaches
(or 1 package frozen peaches)
½ cup sugar
¼ cup melted butter
2 tablespoons brandy or whiskey

Remove crusts from bread, break up into large crumbs. Add hot milk. Cool. When bread has swelled and is soft, add the remaining ingredients. (For the butter, cut 1 quarter-pound stick in half. The measurement does not have to be exact.) If frozen peaches are used, first drain the juice. Pour the thoroughly blended mixture into a buttered baking dish. Bake in a hot oven, 400°F., for 30 minutes.

(The pudding is good either hot or cold. If you want to serve it hot, put it into a cold oven, then turn on the oven after all the guests have arrived, so that it will be baked by the time you sit down to dinner.)

Serve with cream, or garnish with prepared topping just before serving.

STEP 2: Prepare cocktail appetizers. Shrimp Tarragon, Radish Butter Canapés would both be good to precede this meal. Add something crunchy, like salted nuts or Fritos.

STEP 3: Wash the rice, measure salt and water in a saucepan. Leave on back of stove until 20 minutes before dinner is to be served.

STEP 4: Shell the peas. Place in a saucepan on the back of the stove. (Or make Petit Pois à la Francaise.)

STEP 5: Slice tomatoes. Sprinkle with salt from a shaker and scatter tarragon leaves over them. Pour over 1 tablespoon oil and 1 teaspoon lemon juice. Let tomatoes stand in the refrigerator until time to serve.

STEP 6: You will not cook the kidneys until after everyone has arrived, but you can get everything ready beforehand.

KIDNEYS	6 or 7 lamb kidneys
AU FINE CHAMPAGNE	1 tablespoon butter
	1 tablespoon brandy
	2 egg yolks
	1 tablespoon lemon juice
	½ teaspoon salt

Slice the kidneys crosswise, 4 slices to a kidney. Put aside in a bowl. Beat the egg yolks until thick. Squeeze the lemon juice.

When ready to cook the kidneys, while your guests are enjoying a second round of drinks, first melt the butter in a skillet. Add the kidneys, and toss around with a fork or spatula as they brown slightly in the butter. Then add the brandy (*fine champagne* is the distilled liquor similar to cognac which comes from the champagne country of France, but any good brandy or cognac may be used for this dish). Hold the spoon containing the brandy just over the hot kidneys so that liquor will vaporize slightly, then ignite. Burning out the alcohol takes away the harsh character of the brandy, leaving only the flavor. When the alcohol has burned out, add some of the hot sauce to the beaten egg yolks. When smoothly blended, add the lemon juice and salt to the egg mixture, then pour this back into the skillet containing the kidneys. Turn off the fire. The sauce will thicken in what heat is left in the pan. Serve at once.

(If you have a chafing dish, cook the kidneys at the table. It's fun, and impressive, too.)

STEP 7: When the doorbell rings, you should have everything under control. You need only turn the heat on under the rice, cook the peas (or reheat the Petit Pois), and put the salad on the table. If you are going to have hot pudding, you will, of course, turn the oven on about this time. But cooking the kidneys will wait until appetite dictates the approach of the dinner hour.

MENU

Cocktail Appetizers
Kidneys in Sour Cream
Rice   Lima Beans
Tomato and Romaine Salad
Currant Raspberry Fluff   Coffee

FOR FOUR

STEP 1: Prepare the dessert. The Currant Raspberry Fluff must be chilled (not frozen) for at least 2 hours. If left too long in refrigerator before serving, however, it begins to separate.

CURRANT	1 glass currant jelly (¾ cup)
RASPBERRY FLUFF	1 pint fresh or frozen berries
	½ cup confectioners' sugar
	1 egg white, beaten stiff

Beat the egg white until very stiff. Beat the jelly with a spoon until soft, then add gently to the egg white. If frozen berries are used, drain carefully. If fresh berries, add the sugar to them, then stir into the jelly-egg white mixture. With the frozen berries, only ⅓ cup sugar is necessary. Pile into sherbet glasses. Place in colder part of refrigerator until time to serve.

STEP 2: Wash the romaine, cut into serving pieces. Store in refrigerator. Wash tomatoes. Within the last hour before people are due, quarter tomatoes, combine with romaine in bowl which has been rubbed with garlic. Mix dressing at table.

STEP 3: Wash the rice, measure with salt and water in a saucepan. Cook 20 minutes before meal is to be served.

STEP 4: Prepare cocktail appetizers. For something quick and easy, have a Roquefort-cream cheese dip, and stick pretzel sticks in it porcupine fashion. There won't be much of a wait for this meal, once everyone has arrived, so you don't need so much in the way of appetizers.

STEP 5: Use frozen limas, following directions on package.

STEP 6: After everyone has arrived, cook the kidneys.

KIDNEYS IN SOUR CREAM	8 to 10 lamb kidneys, or 2 veal kidneys
	½ clove garlic
	¼ teaspoon oregano
	2 tablespoons butter
	½ teaspoon salt
	¼ cup red wine
	½ cup sour cream

Slice the kidneys crosswise, into 4 or 5 slices for each lamb kidney. (If you use veal kidney, cut into 1-inch pieces.) If you have a chafing dish, this may be cooked at the table. Whatever the utensil used, rub it with the cut garlic clove in advance, then discard the clove. Melt butter, to capture the garlic essence before it has dried.

Five minutes before dinner is to be served, (the rice and limas will already be cooking), reheat the butter, add the sliced kidneys along with the oregano and the salt. Lightly brown the kidneys on both sides. Add the wine. Simmer 3 or 4 minutes. Turn off the heat and add the sour cream. Serve at once.

MENU

Cocktail Appetizers
Kidneys and Mushrooms Chasseur
Rice   Cauliflower
Tomatoes Tarragon
Cantaloupe with Kirsch   Coffee

FOR SIX

STEP 1: Prepare the dessert. For CANTALOUPE WITH KIRSCH, cut the cantaloupe with a melon ball cutter—if you have one. If not, dice the fruit in uniform pieces. Add a little sugar, about ¼ cup (taste the fruit to see if you think it needs more), and ¼ cup kirsch. (If you have no kirsch, you might use another liqueur, or port, or white wine.) Chill in refrigerator. Serve the fruit this way, in sherbet glasses, or with a garnish of vanilla ice cream.

STEP 2: Prepare cocktail appetizers. Garlic Olives and shrimps with Tomato-Horse-radish Sauce would be appropriate.

TOMATO-HORSE-RADISH	½ cup tomato catsup
SAUCE	1 teaspoon lemon juice
	2 teaspoons horse-radish
	¼ teaspoon salt
	¼ teaspoon savory salt (optional)

Cocktail-size shrimp should be used, fresh, frozen, or canned. If fresh, shell them before parboiling. They will curl up as they boil if the shells are removed first. Marinate the shrimp in the sauce, spear with toothpicks to serve. (If you want a more highly seasoned sauce, use the Barbecue Sauce recipe.)

STEP 3: Wash rice, measure with salt and water in saucepan. Cook 20 minutes before dinner is to be served.

STEP 4: Cut cauliflower into flowerlets, and cut the flowerlets into smaller pieces if necessary. Place in saucepan, but do not add water until ready to cook, which will be (as with the rice) 20 minutes before the meal is to be served. Then add boiling water, cook until barely tender, add plenty of butter and a sprinkling of lemon juice.

STEP 5: Slice tomatoes. Sprinkle with salt from a shaker and with taragon leaves. Blend 1 tablespoon oil with 1 teaspoon lemon juice, sprinkle this over tomatoes. Marinate in refrigerator.

STEP 6: Get everything ready for cooking the kidneys, but do not cook them until *after everyone has arrived.*

KIDNEYS AND
MUSHROOMS CHASSEUR

8 lamb kidneys
½ pound smoked sausage
1 tablespoon minced onion
2 tablespoons butter
½ teaspoon salt
½ teaspoon thyme
½ cup sherry
½ cup sour cream
½ pound mushrooms

Slice the kidneys, 4 or 5 slices to each kidney. Slice the smoked sausage into comparable size. Slice the mushrooms if large, use whole if button-size. (Do not peel unless badly colored. The peel adds flavor.) When ready to cook, melt butter in a skillet. Add onion, cook until soft. Add kidneys, brown lightly on each side. Add mushrooms, brown lightly. Then add salt, thyme, smoked sausage. Simmer 3 minutes. Add sherry, boil up to reduce liquid to half. Finally add sour cream after heat has been turned off. Serve at once.

(This is so good, it should win over even the skeptics who were sure they didn't like kidneys.)

MENU

Cocktail Appetizers
Steak and Kidney Pie
Lima Beans   Spinach
Fresh Fruit Sundae   Coffee

FOR SIX

This pie is good either hot or cold. It can be baked ahead of time and served cold if the weather is hot, or reheated just before serving if the weather is cold.

STEP 1: Bake the

<table>
<tr><td>STEAK AND
KIDNEY PIE</td><td>1 pound lean beef, chuck or round
4 or 5 lamb kidneys
1 large or 2 small potatoes
½ cup shelled peas
3 cups meat stock or gravy
½ teaspoon salt
⅛ teaspoon coarse pepper
1 small onion, minced
1 tablespoon minced parsley</td></tr>
<tr><td>CRUST:</td><td>1½ cups flour
½ teaspoon salt
½ teaspoon baking powder
¼ teaspoon soda
¼ cup vegetable shortening
½ cup buttermilk</td></tr>
</table>

First mix the crust, sifting together the flour, salt, baking powder, and soda. Chop in the shortening with a fork, or knife, mincing finely. Add buttermilk slowly, stirring all the while. Knead dough. Divide into two parts. Roll out on floured board, as for pie crust, to about ⅛-inch thickness. Shape the bottom crust around a square baking dish which has been lightly greased.

Now place the beef, cubed, in a layer over the crust. Sprinkle lightly with salt from a shaker. Add a layer of kidneys, sliced thin. Sprinkle more salt, lightly, over the kidneys. Next add a layer of uncooked peas, finely cubed uncooked potato, and minced onion and parsley, mixed together. Sprinkle more salt, still lightly, over the vegetables. Next add another layer of the beef cubes, and if there should be any kidney left, more of the kidney. If you should have any gravy left from another meal, by all means use it, thinning with water if necessary to make 3 cups. Otherwise, make a gravy of 3 tablespoons butter or drippings, 3 tablespoons flour, ½ teaspoon salt, 3 bouillon cubes, 3 cups water (or 1 can of concentrated beef bouillon thinned to make 3 cups, instead of the bouillon cubes and water). Taste for seasoning. When it seems right to you, pour over the meat. Then lay on the top crust, pressing the edges together with the tines of a fork. Cut out a star shape from the center of the crust with a sharp knife. Bake at 350°F. for 1½ hours. Both bottom and top crusts should be golden brown.

STEP 2: Prepare cocktail appetizers. If the oven is to be turned on to reheat the pie, you might have smoked sausage cut in chunks, to slip into the oven to be heated just before serving. Garlic Olives and Cheetos both go well with smoked sausage.

STEP 3: For the dessert, FRESH FRUIT SUNDAE, serve blueberries, peaches, or bananas, or a combination of the three, over vanilla ice cream. Frozen peaches, or canned "home style" peaches are both good, because they are soft and the sirup blends well with the vanilla flavor of the ice cream. Blueberries should be sugared in advance, or may be cooked slightly, in a sirup of sugar and water, then chilled. Bananas should be cut lengthwise only a few minutes before the scheduled dinner hour. Keep ice cream in freezing compartment of refrigerator until dessert is wanted.

STEP 4: If you use both frozen limas and frozen spinach, you need allow only 5 minutes for getting the two vegetables cooked. Place in saucepan, add salt. Add boiling water when ready to cook.

STEP 5: Set table. Put coffee and water in pot. Get dressed. Try one of your cocktails.

STEP 6: After people have come, turn on the oven, reheat the pie (unless you're having it cold) during the first round of cocktails. Heat the smoked sausage at the same time, but only for 5 minutes. Turn the heat on under the teakettle, so you'll have plenty of boiling water when ready to cook the limas and spinach.

EGGS
for a
Late Supper

MENU

Cocktail Appetizers
Simple Omelet
Asparagus on Toast
Tomato and Lettuce Salad
Strawberry Tarts   Coffee

FOR FOUR

Making an omelet is the simplest thing in the world—yet how rare it is to have a really perfect omelet. Once learned, the secret is always yours, and you can always produce a delicious meal on the spur of the moment. Omelets can be varied in a dozen different ways. Fill them with vegetables, meat or fish—or spaghetti. Or grated cheese. Pour a sauce over the omelet: tomato, cheese, or brown Chinese sauce. Or combine with sausage, ham, bacon, grilled kidneys, or grilled chicken livers.

But never be ashamed to offer a perfectly simple omelet, unadorned, delicate, tender, fresh from the pan.

STEP 1: Prepare the dessert.

STRAWBERRY TARTS   4 baked tart shells
Currant jelly
1 pint fresh strawberries, sugared

Bake the tart shells, using your favorite recipe for pastry dough or a prepared mix. One cup flour is enough; divide the dough into 4 portions to roll out. Bake in individual tart pans, or over inverted muffin cups.

When cool, place ripe, perfect strawberries in each tart shell, hulled but left whole. Sprinkle granulated sugar over the berries, 1 tablespoonful of sugar for each tart. Then put currant jelly in a saucepan, hold it over medium heat until the jelly has softened, then place enough of the jelly over the uncooked berries to form a glaze. Place in refrigerator until jelly has hardened again. Delicious—the best strawberry tarts you ever tasted!

(When strawberries are not in season, you can do the same thing with frozen raspberries. Drain the berries first, then place them in the tart shells before they've had a chance to become very soft.)

STEP 2: Prepare cocktail appetizers. Cocktail frankfurters in Barbecue Sauce would be a good choice. The sauce may be mixed 24 hours in advance, the frankfurters marinated in it, then heated just before serving.

STEP 3: Clean asparagus thoroughly by scrubbing with a stiff brush to loosen all grit. Cut off stalks at point where they start to become tough. Plan to cook 5 minutes before dinner is to be served in a skillet so that the spears can be laid out flat, or standing upright in the top of a double boiler. Use only ½ cup water, a scant ¼ teaspoon salt. Take the asparagus out of the water as soon as tender (some spears take longer to cook than others). Lay on toast, pour over the toast a teaspoon of the liquor in which the asparagus cooked, and dot each serving with a generous piece of butter.

STEP 4: Wash lettuce. Slice fine. Store in refrigerator. Make a Russian dressing of mayonnaise, catsup, and finely chopped pickles. Just before serving, mix the sliced head lettuce and quartered tomatoes with the Russian dressing.

STEP 5: Set table. Put coffee and water in pot. Get yourself ready.

STEP 6: After everyone has come and cocktails and appetizers are being enjoyed, cook the asparagus, toast the toast, and make the

OMELET

Use 1 egg for each person. Break eggs into a large bowl. Beat with a wire whisk or a fork, lifting up your wrist in a cupping motion, getting as much air into the eggs as possible. As you beat, add a scant ¼ teaspoon salt, 2 tablespoons milk for 4 eggs.

Now melt butter in the skillet or omelet pan. If you have a special omelet pan, ½ tablespoon of butter is enough. More butter may be necessary if you are using an ordinary skillet. (If you like scrambled eggs and omelets, it will pay you to buy an omelet pan, one with a rounded bottom. Never wash this pan. Clean it by rubbing vigorously with successive pieces of paper towel until there is no trace of grease left. Use the pan only for eggs, nothing else. If treated properly, you will never have trouble with omelets sticking to this pan.)

When the butter is melted, gently pour in the beaten eggs. Lower the heat to simmering. Stand over the pan constantly until the omelet is finished, lifting up with a spatula as the crust forms on the bottom and around the edge. Twist and turn the pan so that the liquid on top rolls over to the side, and can then be allowed to run under as you lift the forming omelet.

As soon as the omelet is solid, only moist on top, lift up to see whether it is golden on the bottom. Do not turn up the heat to hasten cooking. That will only toughen the omelet. Be patient. The egg will form a golden crust in a matter of minutes. Then fold over, still using a gentle motion, and slip out onto a platter. Or, you may cut the omelet into serving portions before removing from the pan. Serve immediately, on plates warmed in the oven.

MENU

Cocktail Appetizers
Oeuf au Plat
Garlic Bread
Green Salad with Roquefort Dressing
Chocolate Pudding   Coffee

FOR SIX

This solves the problem of a hastily put together meal after an all-day outing, or a spontaneous Sunday-night get-together.

STEP 1: For dessert make CHOCOLATE PUDDING, using a prepared mix. Instead of whipped cream on top, you might use pistachio or butter pecan ice cream, picked up at the last minute from the drug store, or kept in the freezing compartment of your refrigerator. Other variations: garnish with chopped pistachio nuts, or with toasted coconut, or with sliced bananas and cream.

STEP 2: For cocktail appetizers, you might mix an Anchovy-Chive Cheese Paste, to be served on crackers or as a dunk for potato chips.

ANCHOVY-CHIVE	1 tin anchovy fillets
CHEESE PASTE	Chive cheese
	1 tablespoon capers

Mash the fillets. Add an equal quantity of chive cheese. Then add capers, and mash all together into a smooth paste.

STEP 3: Wash salad greens. Cut into serving portions. Store in refrigerator. Mix dressing, add finely crumbled Roquefort or other blue cheese to French dressing.

STEP 4: For the GARLIC BREAD, cut French bread into thick slices, at a 45° angle, cutting only part way through the loaf. Melt ¼ pound butter, or half butter and half margarine, adding 2 or 3 cloves of sliced garlic. Remove the garlic before spreading butter on bread. Brush the melted butter over the gashes in the bread. Later, just before supper is to be served, place the bread in a hot oven until slightly toasted.

STEP 5: OEUF AU PLAT requires only 10 minutes' cooking time, if the oven is already heated, so you can wait to put the eggs into the oven until people seem ready to eat. Place a dab of butter, about 1 tea-spoonful, into each individual ramekin. Slip into the hot oven, 450°F., for 2 or 3 minutes. Then remove, break 2 eggs into each dish, add a little milk or cream, and sprinkle with salt from a shaker and with monosodium glutamate (this is optional). Put the ramekins back into the oven. Bake until the white is cooked through, but the yolk still soft. This should not be more than 10 minutes. Serve immediately.

Any number of variations are possible. Oeuf Plat au Jambon is the French ham and eggs. A very thin slice of ham goes into the ramekin first, then the eggs are broken over this. Sometimes a well-seasoned tomato sauce is poured over the eggs. Or, again, grated cheese may be sprinkled over the top. Still another variation is to place fresh shrimp in the ramekins with a few slices of onion previously softened in butter. Eggs will be broken over the shrimp, and the two cooked to-gether.

Most important is to cook the eggs until the white is solid, not a second longer.

STEP 6: During the 10 minutes required for the eggs to cook, and while the Garlic Bread is being toasted, mix the salad greens in a garlic-rubbed bowl, and add the dressing. Start the coffee, and have plenty of it. A satisfying repast, indeed.

MENU

Cocktail Appetizers
Ham 'n' Eggs
Lyonnaise Potatoes   Tomatoes Tarragon
Ginger Cookies   Coffee

FOR SIX

Once I saw on a phonetically spelled menu in the Serbian part of Yugoslavia the item "emenex." This, I was told upon inquiry, was an American dish. They were surprised I didn't know it. "Emenex?" Why, nothing else but Ham 'n' Eggs!

This good old American stand-by can be delicious, too, though like everything else, it needs loving preparation. The ham must be lean and tender, the eggs cooked over lowest heat. Then serve it up proudly, for there's nothing better.

STEP 1: Prepare the dessert. Bake GINGER COOKIES, using prepared gingerbread mix, following directions on the package. These will keep almost indefinitely, so that they can be made 24 hours—or more —in advance.

STEP 2: Prepare cocktail appetizers—or buy them. If this is to be a spur-of-the-moment meal, as it probably will be, get such ready-to-serve things as cheese popcorn, pretzels, stuffed olives, or Fritos.

STEP 3: Slice tomatoes. Scatter with tarragon leaves and sprinkle with salt from a shaker. Then pour over them a mixture of 1 tablespoon olive oil and 1 teaspoon of lemon juice. Marinate in refrigerator until ready to serve.

STEP 4: Set table. Put coffee and water in pot. Perhaps you will want to serve coffee with this meal. If so turn the heat on under the coffee as the potatoes cook.

STEP 5: For the LYONNAISE POTATOES, peel and slice 5 medium potatoes and 2 or 3 medium onions. Twenty minutes before dinner is to be served, heat 2 tablespoons fat (bacon drippings, preferably) in a skillet, then add the thinly sliced potatoes and onions. Sprinkle over them ½ teaspoon salt and ¼ teaspoon paprika. Cover. Turn the heat low. Every now and then turn over with a spatula to prevent potatoes or onions burning, but put the cover back on immediately, until the potatoes are tender.

STEP 6: As the potatoes cook, start the ham for the HAM 'N' EGGS. Melt 1 tablespoon butter in a skillet. Place the slices of ham, cut into 6 serving portions, in the melted butter. For 6 people, you will need 2 pounds of ham, cut from the center, but sliced thin. If not all the ham will go into the skillet at once, remove each piece after it has browned on both sides, to a platter, then add the remaining pieces. When you have finished cooking the ham, break the eggs into the skillet, letting them cook in the ham fat and essence remaining in the pan. Allow at least 1 egg to a person. If your guests have been out in the wind and are obviously ravenous, better give them 2 eggs apiece. Sprinkle the eggs lightly with salt from a shaker. Cover the skillet for 2 minutes, to steam the eggs, then remove the cover to prevent the yolks from glazing over. Cook until the white is just solid through (keep the heat low under the skillet throughout) and the yolks still soft. Serve at once. Scoop up all the essence in the pan and pour over the eggs. This is the best part of all.

Have plenty of bread, either French bread or crusty rolls, for the proper way to eat Ham 'n' Eggs is to use bread for scooping up the egg yolk mixed with ham essence. If you must be dainty about it, spear the bread with a fork as you wipe up the plate. As the hostess (or host) you set the pace, and your guests will all be grateful if they see you doing what they would like to do themselves.

MENU

Cocktail Appetizers
Spanish Omelet with Onions and Potatoes
Avocado Salad
Figs in Wine   Coffee

FOR SIX

STEP 1: Prepare the dessert.

FIGS IN WINE

1 pound dried figs
1 cup water
2 cups white wine
1 tablespoon lemon juice
Cream

Either the preceding day, or early in the morning, cover figs with wine. Soak 4 hours or more. Add lemon juice, and water, place in saucepan, and bring to a boil. Simmer, covered, for 30 minutes, or until figs are tender. Uncover. Cook more briskly for 5 minutes, reducing the liquid. Cool. Pour into dessert dishes. Chill in refrigerator until dessert time. At table, pass cream to be poured over figs.

STEP 2: Prepare cocktail appetizers. Grilled Cheese Canapés and shrimps in Tomato Cream Sauce would make excellent appetizers for this meal. The cheese mixture can be spread on either crackers or melba toast rounds hours in advance, then placed under the broiler as you pour out the first cocktails. The shrimps can be prepared 24 hours in advance, and will be better for marinating in the sauce that long.

STEP 3: For the AVOCADO SALAD, mix French dressing. Plan to serve the avocado halves on a bed of water cress, or on finely sliced head lettuce, the dressing poured into the seed cavity of the avocado. Place on individual plates, and put on the table a short time before guests are due.

STEP 4: Set table. Put coffee and water in pot. Get yourself ready.

STEP 5: Prepare ingredients for the omelet, but do not cook until after everyone has come.

SPANISH OMELET

- 2 cups diced potatoes
- 1 cup sliced onions
- 6 eggs
- 2 tablespoons olive oil or sweet butter
- ⅛ teaspoon black pepper
- Salt

Peel and dice the potatoes very fine. Peel and slice the onions. *After everyone is present*, heat the oil or butter in an omelet pan or skillet (an 8-inch pan will be the right size), shaking so that every inch of the skillet is covered. Keep heat as low as possible. Add potatoes and onions to the hot oil (or butter), chopping with a spatula all the time the vegetables cook, to cut them into finely minced particles, at the same time mixing the onion and potato thoroughly together. Sprinkle salt from a shaker lightly over the vegetables as they cook. When both potatoes and onions have softened, beat the 6 eggs in a large bowl, using either a wire whisk or an egg beater. Add a scant ¼ teaspoon of salt and pepper. Pour a third of the eggs into the pan. As soon as any crust forms, start lifting up with the spatula, to let the liquid run under, and cut grooves in the center for the same purpose. When the omelet is nearly solid, and a golden crust has formed on the bottom, hold a plate over the skillet, one large enough to cover completely, then turn the omelet upside down, just as when you turn out an upside down cake. Scrape out the omelet pan carefully. If necessary, add a little more oil or sweet butter, about a teaspoonful, to keep the pan slick. Slide the omelet back into the pan, with the crust side uppermost. Add the second third of eggs. Do exactly as before. When a golden crust has again formed on the bottom, turn the omelet out again on the plate and again return with the golden side uppermost. Add the remainder of beaten egg, and repeat the entire process. This time, when a golden crust has formed on the bottom, turn out upside down and serve immediately, cutting into pie-shaped wedges.

The result of this slow cooking of layer after layer of omelet is a deliciously nutty flavor. It's an excellent choice for an after-theater supper, or an evening when you have impulsively asked friends home for supper with you. The preparation is complicated. You had better try it out on the family first to practice. Altogether 30 to 35 minutes is required for the actual cooking. Ask your guests to come into the kitchen while you cook the omelet, and serve apéritifs there. Such informality is part of the pattern of today's living, and most people love it.

MENU

Cocktail Appetizers
Eggs Foo Yong
Brussels Sprouts with Pork
Peach-Orange Ambrosia   Tea or Coffee

FOR SIX

There's a trick to making Eggs Foo Yong, and you'd better practice on the family before trying to serve this dish to company. However, once learned, you can serve this Chinese form of omelet with pride, for it's delicious (and surprisingly inexpensive).

STEP 1: Get everything ready for cooking the Eggs Foo Yong, but do not actually cook the eggs until everyone is present.

EGGS FOO YONG

2 scallions, minced
¼ cup minced celery
½ cup mushrooms, sliced
¼ cup cooked peas, or
    other cooked vegetable
½ cup crabmeat, minced chicken,
    pork, shrimp, or ham
1 tablespoon soy sauce
4 eggs
4 tablespoons oil

The above is merely a suggestion of possible ingredients. Any leftovers in the refrigerator may be utilized. Both the celery and the scallions add greatly to the flavor, and I suggest you include these every time. But decide on the ingredients otherwise according to what you have.

Mince everything very fine. Only foods already cooked will go into the Foo Yong. Cut up the scallions, mushrooms, and celery (slice the celery at an angle to make it paper-thin) and cook, covered, for 2 or 3 minutes in 2 tablespoons oil or butter. Put aside. Put each of the other vegetables, and the sea food or meat, into separate bowls. Now make

CHINESE BROWN SAUCE

1 teaspoon cornstarch
2 teaspoons soy sauce
¼ teaspoon sugar
¼ teaspoon dry mustard
½ cup water

Mix the first four ingredients to a paste, then add water. Boil until thick and clear (about 3 or 4 minutes). Put aside.

Just before dinner is to be served, put about ½ tablespoon of oil in an omelet pan or small skillet. Shake until every bit of the pan is covered with oil. Heat. Beat the eggs until light, add the chopped-up vegetables and the sea food (or meat, or chicken), and the soy sauce. Drop 2 heaping tablespoons of the egg mixture into the hot pan. Cook as if these were pancakes, lifting up to see when the Foo Yong is browned all over the bottom. Then turn over with a spatula or pancake turner and brown on the other side. This is the part that is tricky. If one small part is not browned, the Foo Yong may fall apart when you lift it. Don't let this dismay you. After a few false starts you'll see how to do it, and those which do crumble will taste perfectly all right, they simply do not look as beautiful as the others.

Finally, after removing the Foo Yong from the pan, pour a little of the Brown Sauce over each serving. This recipe should make 6 individual "pancakes."

STEP 2: The BRUSSELS SPROUTS WITH PORK, like the Foo Yong, will not be completed until just before dinner. You can finish this while the Foo Yong browns. Everything will be carefully prepared and partially cooked in advance.

Trim the brussels sprouts, remove all traces of discoloration, then cover with boiling water. Add salt, cook for 5 minutes. Meantime, slice the lean from 1 or 2 pork chops with a sharp knife, making slivers about 1 inch in length, ¼ inch in width. Cook the pork in 1 tablespoon of oil in a skillet, turning to brown on all sides. Combine the drained brussels sprouts with the pork, add 1 teaspoon soy sauce. Leave in the skillet. Just before serving, cook the sprouts and pork together for another 2 minutes.

STEP 3: Prepare the dessert. For PEACH-ORANGE AMBROSIA, cut oranges into small pieces. Combine with sliced peaches, fresh or frozen. Add sugar, and sprinkle grated coconut over the top. Chill in the refrigerator until ready to serve.

STEP 4: Prepare cocktail appetizers. Appropriate for this meal would be

STEAMED GINGER SHRIMP ½ pound shrimp
           2 tablespoons shredded ginger
           ¼ cup dry white wine
           1 tablespoon soy sauce

Shell and de-vein shrimp. Mince ginger root very fine, combine with wine and soy sauce. Marinate shrimp in this. After everyone is present, heat the shrimp in the marinade for about 5 minutes, or until pink. Serve hot, speared with toothpicks.

194

Even without the ginger this is good. You could substitute 2 table-spoons of finely minced scallion or chives.

STEP 5: While your guests are enjoying cocktails, make the Foo Yong, reheat the brussels sprouts and pork, and brew the tea. Be sure to have the teapot boiling-hot before you add the tea leaves, and be sure that the teakettle is steaming like an engine before you pour water on the leaves. It makes a world of difference.

Smörgåsbord Waits for All Men

MENU

Lobster with Sweet Pickle Sauce
Poached Salmon with Lemon   Sardines
Olives   Swiss Cheese   Beet Salad
Hot Broiled Meat Balls in Barbecue Sauce
Tomatoes Tarragon   Green Salad
Macaroni and Cheese
Ice Cream with Peach Rum Sauce
Cookies   Coffee

FOR TWENTY

When it's necessary to entertain a crowd, the best way to do it is to serve smörgåsbord. Virtually everything can be set out long in advance, for you need have only one hot dish. This means a lot of advance preparation, but it so greatly lessens the frenzy of trying to get hot food to everybody at once that it's worth what extra labor is involved. This way, you put everything on a buffet, or any large table, and let people help themselves. Drinks are set out on another table, and there's self-service there, too. Gives you a chance to enjoy your guests.

STEP 1: Order a gallon of ice cream from the confectionery (or the drug store) to be delivered in a bucket of ice at whatever hour you guess people will be ready for dessert. If they are invited for six-thirty, they will probably start helping themselves from the buffet about seven, or quarter past. Dessert will not be needed until eight. Even if some people are ready for dessert before that time, don't worry. You've given them plenty to satisfy their appetites. Eight-thirty may be soon enough for dessert. You will probably know your guests well enough to judge by past performances.

STEP 2: Make the Peach Rum Sauce for the ice cream, tripling the recipe given previously.

STEP 3: Cook African lobster tails for the LOBSTER WITH SWEET PICKLE SAUCE. Four lobster tails should be enough, since this is only one of many dishes. Parboil the lobster in boiling water about 10 minutes, or until the flesh turns pink. Avoid overcooking. Then with a sharp knife, slice lobster meat into thin pieces. The sauce is the same as that for Lobster Salad Canapés but triple the quantity. Lay the lobster slices neatly on a small platter, then mask with the sauce. Keep this in refrigerator until shortly before guests are due.

STEP 4: A whole salmon, poached in Court Bouillon, is an impressive and delicious addition to any buffet. If you can buy the fresh salmon from a local fish market, do try this. For POACHED SALMON, first prepare a Court Bouillon. Strain. Reheat. Gently lower the salmon into the kettle. (You may first wrap the salmon in cheesecloth for easier handling.) Be sure you have liquid enough to cover. Simmer gently, allowing 12 minutes to the pound. When done, pour off part of the Court Bouillon, then remove the salmon to a platter. Serve cold with lemon wedges around the platter and a bowl of well-seasoned mayonnaise near by. You may add capers and finely chopped red pepper (or pimiento) to the mayonnaise, if you prefer.

Suppose you can't buy fresh salmon? Then buy 2 cans of the finest quality salmon you can find. Open the cans carefully, so that the salmon can be removed without its breaking up. Slice down the center with a sharp knife, and arrange on a plate with the rounded side up. Keep chilled in refrigerator until ready to serve.

STEP 5: Cook the macaroni for MACARONI AND CHEESE. For 20 people, plan to bake 2 large casseroles. This is the one hot dish, and the only one of which you must have 20 full servings. Two pounds of macaroni should be enough. Make plenty of cream sauce, about 3 cups of it for each casserole. (Thin with additional milk, if necessary, to cover macaroni in the dish.) Get 1 pound of sharp cheese, and cut the cheese into cubes, then add to the sauce as it is cooking. In this way, the cheese will be thoroughly blended. When there are so many other intricate flavors in the meal, it seems to me the macaroni should be kept simple. However, you may add slices of ham, or shrimp, or cut-up chicken to the casserole, if you like. Top with fine bread crumbs thoroughly mixed with grated cheese and dotted with butter. Put the casseroles in a cold oven. Turn on the oven to 350°F. about the time people are due, allowing 40 minutes to 1 hour for baking.

STEP 6: Parboil beets for the BEET SALAD. Every self-respecting smörgåsbord has at least one dish of beet salad. Not exciting, but it helps to balance the rich fare. Cook the beets with skins on, until tender when pricked with a fork. (Or use canned beets.) Let them get cold enough to handle, then peel and slice or cube. For the dressing, use

> 1 teaspoon sugar
> 1 teaspoon salt
> 1 teaspoon grated onion and juice
> 1 tablespoon vinegar

This is enough for 2 bunches, or 1 can of beets. You might also slice sweet red onion and combine with the beets. Garnish with fresh dill.

STEP 7: For the MEAT BALLS IN BARBECUE SAUCE prepare the meat balls so that they are ready to slip under the broiler. Get 2 pounds ground chuck, blend it with 1½ teaspoons salt, ½ teaspoon oregano. Form into tiny balls, ½ to ¾ inch in diameter. Place on a pan that can be slipped under broiler for 5 minutes before they are to be served.

Make Barbecue Sauce. Serve this hot over the meat balls. Keep them in a baking dish with cover, so that they will keep warm as long as possible.

STEP 8: Wash salad greens—and have plenty of them. Two heads of romaine, a bunch of water cress, and some curly chicory would just about supply the need. Store in plastic bags in refrigerator, already cut to serving size. Mix with French dressing within the last hour before guests are due.

STEP 9: Slice tomatoes for TOMATOES TARRAGON. Sprinkle with salt from a shaker, with tarragon leaves, and with a mixture of olive oil and lemon juice, mixed 3 parts oil to 1 of lemon juice. Marinate the tomato slices in this dressing, in the refrigerator.

STEP 10: Open the sardines, and lay out on a platter like spokes from a wheel with lemon wedges and sprigs of parsley here and there.

STEP 11: Cut cheese in cubes. Arrange on a platter with black olives piled up at either end.

STEP 12: Set the table. As for coffee, it's unlikely that you have a coffeepot large enough to brew 20 cups at once. Plan what you will do about this problem. You might make instant coffee, then you will only have to boil a kettleful of water. Or, you might borrow a coffeepot from the neighbors.

STEP 13: Get yourself dressed and in the right mood.

STEP 14: Within the last half hour before guests are expected, put all the cold food out on the buffet. Reheat the Barbecue Sauce for the broiled meat balls and keep warm. After the doorbell rings and you have properly greeted the first guests, turn on the oven for the macaroni. You need not put the meat balls under the broiler until after the first round of drinks has been served. Since the oven will already be turned on, the meat balls will cook very quickly—so quickly, you'd better stay and watch them and not let yourself get distracted by something else. Pour the hot Barbecue Sauce over the meat balls before taking them to the buffet.

By the time you carry the hot casseroles of macaroni to the table, the party should already be gay. If the ice cream has not yet arrived, give the store a call. Have the Peach Rum Sauce ready, and the dessert dishes out. Have cookies in a bowl. Start the water boiling for coffee.

It's a big undertaking to entertain so many at once, but with efficient planning you should carry the whole thing off easily.

Don't give a thought yet to the dishes to be cleared up. Let tomorrow take care of that!

MENU

Shrimp with Tomato-Horseradish Sauce
Smoked Swordfish   Herring Salad
Sliced Ham, Orange Sauce
Stuffed Baked Tomatoes   Cucumbers with Dill
Roast Turkey, Almond-Chestnut Dressing
Green Salad   Hot Rolls
Blackberry Jam Layer Cake   Coffee

FOR TWENTY

You don't have to have as many as 20 people when you serve smörgåsbord. Perhaps you'll want to do it for a mere dozen. In that case, don't have more than four things besides the one important hot dish. However, the chief virtue of the smörgåsbord idea is for serving a large crowd. This particular menu is appropriate for the Christmas holiday season, though it could be served at almost any time of the year.

STEP 1: A turkey is beautiful to look at, easy to prepare, and everybody likes it. To make it a little out of the ordinary, stuff it with

ALMOND-CHESTNUT
DRESSING

1 large loaf white bread
½ pound chestnuts
½ pound almonds, chopped
2 tablespoons minced parsley
2 scallions, minced
½ teaspoon sage
¼ teaspoon marjoram
¼ teaspoon thyme
¼ teaspoon mace
1 tablespoon salt

Parboil the chestnuts 15 minutes, or until tender. Cool. Peel off shell with a sharp knife. Slice fine. Use the shelled almonds, cut small without blanching. Mix these and the remaining ingredients together. Stuff into the turkey, both the neck cavity and the breast cavity, and sew up. This is enough dressing for a 15-pound bird.

The turkey can be put into a cold oven the night before—especially if it is a frozen bird and needs to be thoroughly thawed. If not frozen, partially roast the turkey the preceding night, and finish the job during the afternoon before the party.

Time the roasting so that the turkey is done about an hour (but not much more than that) before guests are due. Remove turkey from roaster and make gravy, lots of it. Slice the meat from one half the bird, and remove as much of the dressing as possible without tearing the bird apart. You may slice the bird up entirely, and take out all the dressing, but the sight of even half that gloriously golden bird delights most people. After the turkey has been sliced, and the gravy made, the turkey can be replaced in the roaster and reheated about the time people are due.

The dressing, in particular, should be kept as warm as possible, and the gravy should be served to the company piping-hot. These, and the baked tomatoes, will be the only hot foods.

STEP 2: Buy an imported Danish or Dutch ham, a 5-pound one, for a buffet offering that is reliably delicious, succulent, and free of waste. Remove ham from the can, and bake in the oven with the following sauce:

ORANGE SAUCE	1 teaspoon prepared mustard
FOR HAM	2 tablespoons sugar
	½ teaspoon powdered cloves
	1 cup orange juice

Scrape all the gelatin out of the can. Place around the ham in the roasting pan. Spread mustard over the fat side of the ham. Sprinkle the sugar and powdered cloves, mixed together, over the mustard. Pour the orange juice, made from frozen concentrate, over all. Bake 30 minutes at 375°F. Remove ham to platter, pour sauce on top. Chill. Slice after ham has been in refrigerator 3 or 4 hours. The orange-flavored gelatin makes a delicious sauce, either hot or cold. You might heat it after people have come and serve it in a sauce boat beside the ham, even though the ham itself is cold.

STEP 3: Prepare the dessert. It might be a good idea to bake 2 cakes, to be sure you have enough, and in that case make 2 different kinds. Blackberry Jam Layer Cake is certainly a festive offering for one. Fudge Cake is a never failing favorite for the other. With all the mixes available these days, for both cake and frosting, cake baking is no longer much of a chore.

STEP 4: Prepare Tomato-Horse-radish Sauce for shrimp. Use either canned, frozen, or fresh shrimp. With all the work making demands on your time, canned shrimp is certainly the easiest.

STEP 5: Prepare the tomatoes, but do not put into the oven to bake until after the first guests have arrived.

STUFFED BAKED TOMATOES

20 medium tomatoes
3 tablespoons fat or oil
1½ pounds ground meat
1¼ teaspoons salt
½ cup chopped onion
1 or 2 garlic cloves, minced
1½ teaspoons thyme
1½ teaspoons minced parsley
1 or 2 bay leaves
1 cup bread crumbs

Heat fat or oil in a skillet. Add minced garlic and onion, cook until soft but not brown. Add meat, stir around until well coated. Add salt, herbs, and finally the bread crumbs. Scoop out the centers from the tomatoes (save centers for making tomato sauce or soup). Stuff with the meat-bread-herb mixture. Pour a little olive oil, about 1½ tablespoons, in the bottom of the roasting pan or casserole you plan to use for the tomatoes. Place the stuffed tomatoes as close together as possible in the pan. *After guests have arrived,* place in oven set at 350°F. and bake for 30 to 35 minutes. Garnish with fresh sprigs of water cress. (For 6 people, divide ingredients for the stuffing by one third, with 1 clove garlic. Exact proportions do not matter.)

STEP 6: Slice cucumbers paper-thin. Marinate in vinegar and salt. For 2 large cucumbers, you will need 3 tablespoons vinegar, ½ teaspoon salt. Sprinkle fresh dill, chopped fine, over the top. (If you can't get fresh dill, use finely minced parsley.)

STEP 7: Scandinavian-type herring salad, consisting of herring fillets, sliced onion, and spices in brine, is available in jars, and is so good there is no point in trying to make it yourself. Simply arrange it in a bowl and decorate with finely minced parsley. Herring salad, like beet salad, is standard fare in every Swedish smörgåsbord.

STEP 8: Smoked swordfish also comes in cans, but the best is the kind you buy by the quarter pound at very fancy delicatessens. Very rich, so you don't need to buy more than half a pound, even for a crowd. Have it sliced very thin.

STEP 9: Cut salad greens into serving portions. Wash carefully. Store in refrigerator. Add any cooked vegetables to the salad which you happen to have left over in the refrigerator, or cut-up green pepper, tomatoes, olives, or any other vegetables you happen to like in the raw state. Prepare the dressing now, but do not add to salad until the last minute.

STEP 10: Set table. Get everything ready for making coffee, planning how you can brew as many as 20 cups of it. Put the rolls in a pan that can be slipped into the oven at the last minute. Pocketbook rolls, with a dab of butter put into the pocket before they are placed in the oven, are very satisfactory for a party like this. No knives needed for spreading butter. Order them especially from the bakery.

STEP 11: The turkey will probably have been in the oven for several hours by now. Test it for doneness. If the thigh seems tender, remove the turkey from the roaster and make the gravy. Scoop out dressing as deftly as you can.

STEP 12: Get yourself dressed. Just before people are due to arrive, set out most of the cold dishes on the buffet. After the first few guests have come, put the tomatoes in the oven to bake, and see that the remaining cold dishes are on the buffet. Put the salad together. Slip the rolls into the oven to heat. Bring the half-carved turkey out to set on the table after everyone has arrived.

MENU

Crabmeat Salad
Herring in Sour Cream   Smoked Salmon
Assorted Cheeses   Liver Pâté
Radishes, Tomatoes, Celery, Olives
Hot Smoked Sausage
Hash Pie
Assorted Breads
Frozen Fruit Compote   Coffee

FOR TWENTY

STEP 1: Several days in advance, prepare

LIVER PÂTÉ

1 pound liverwurst
⅛ teaspoon thyme
1 tablespoon Worcestershire
sauce
⅛ teaspoon mace
¼ cup sweet butter
1 teaspoon powdered cloves
1½ tablespoons sherry
1 tablespoon grated onion and juice
¼ teaspoon black pepper

Get the best quality liverwurst. Remove the skin. Beat up with a wooden spoon, until very creamy. Powder the dried thyme by rubbing through the fingers. Add the Worcestershire, the spices, the onion juice, sherry, and the butter which has been softened to the consistency of whipped cream. Mash this mixture well together until it is a fine paste. Pour into a nice-looking crock. Press waxed paper down over the top to keep it moist. Keep in the refrigerator until ready to serve. The longer it stands the better the flavor. Call it your "Pâté Maison," in the manner of French restaurants.

STEP 2: On the day of the party, mix the

CRABMEAT SALAD

2 cans crabmeat
1 cup mayonnaise
2 tablespoons catsup
1 teaspoon horse-radish
1 tablespoon lemon juice
¼ teaspoon salt (about)
1 cup chopped cucumber
½ cup chopped celery
½ teaspoon prepared mustard
1 teaspoon minced fresh parsley
1 avocado
Lettuce

Flake the crabmeat, removing all gristle. Make a sauce of mayonnaise, catsup, horse-radish, mustard, lemon juice, and parsley. Add salt, taste to see whether you think it's enough. Peel cucumber, chop very fine. Cut celery as small as possible. Combine crabmeat, cucumber, and celery with the sauce. Keep in refrigerator until shortly before guests are due, then arrange on a platter or plate, on cupped lettuce leaves, and decorate with slices of avocado.

STEP 3: Start preparing

HASH PIE

3 pounds ground meat
4 medium potatoes
4 medium onions
3 tablespoons bacon fat
1¾ teaspoons salt
3 bouillon cubes
½ cup sherry
3 cups water
4 tablespoons catsup
1 green pepper (optional)

Melt the fat in a large skillet. Add the ground meat, which may be all beef, hamburger type, or a combination of beef and pork. Stir the meat around in the hot fat, then add the potatoes and onions, both peeled and very finely chopped. If green pepper is added, chop it very fine. With a knife, continue to chop the meat and vegetables as the mixture simmers, just as for regular beef hash. Add salt, catsup, and sherry, and simmer gently for 5 minutes. Add water and bouillon cubes. Cover. Simmer 15 or 20 minutes.

Meantime, make the crust, using the same recipe as the crust for Steak and Kidney Pie. Divide dough in half. Roll out very thin.

The above recipe is enough for 2 casseroles, one to be set on each end of the buffet (or only one put on the table at a time, the second being brought out to replace the first). This crust recipe should be enough to top 2 casseroles, but that will depend on whether the casseroles tend to be low and very wide or deeper and not so wide. You may have to make up a second batch of dough.

Cut out crescents or star shapes from the crust. Leave the casserole dishes in a cold oven until guests start to arrive. Then turn on to 350°F. and bake about 30 minutes, or until crust is golden.

Moussaka is also good for a smörgåsbord, though its preparation is more complicated.

STEP 4: Prepare the dessert—or at least get the ingredients ready, so it can be put together easily at the last minute. A compote of several frozen fruits, flavored with wine or liqueur, is easy to prepare, easy to serve, and sure to please everybody. You will need 5 packages of frozen fruit for 20 people. A good combination would be 2 packages of sliced peaches, 2 of strawberries, 1 of loganberries. A can of bartlett pears might also be added, the pears sliced or cubed first. Peaches, raspberries, and blueberries make another excellent combination.

Place the packages of frozen fruit in the refrigerator, but not in the freezing compartment. Do not open until ready to serve dessert. Then combine all together in a large bowl, fruit, juice, and everything. Add 1 cup white wine, such as sauterne, or ½ cup of a liqueur such as Cointreau. Serve from the bowl into sherbet glasses, or punch cups rented for the occasion.

STEP 5: Trim radishes and celery. Arrange in bowl with olives. Keep in refrigerator. Slice tomatoes during the last hour before setting the food out, sprinkle salt over the tomato slices, then a French dressing with a little Roquefort cheese crumbled into it.

STEP 6: Everything else needed for the buffet can be bought ready to serve. Herring in sour cream comes in jars, and is delicious just as it is. Smoked salmon will come either out of cans, or from the delicatessen, already sliced. Smoked sausage will also come from the delicatessen. Cut it into 1- or 2-inch lengths and slip under the broiler just before serving it.

STEP 7: Set the table. Plan how you're going to prepare coffee for 20 people. Get yourself dressed.

STEP 8: During the last 15 or 20 minutes before people are due, put all the cold dishes on the buffet. When the first guests arrive, turn on the oven as you go out to fix drinks for them. Slip the smoked sausage under the broiler unit to heat. Leave the Hash Pie in the oven for 30 to 45 minutes, until the crust is golden. Then you can enjoy the party too, with no further concern until it's time to put the frozen fruit together for the dessert.

INDEX

214

MENU FOR SAFETY

A good cook is a safe cook. A good cook knows that danger lurks in the kitchen. Burns, caused by stoves and grates, account for more than one third of all home accidents, with women and children the major sufferers. The Menu for Safety is one menu that the good cook follows every day and uses in preparing every meal. It has only two simple ingredients—Prevention and Preparedness—but knowledge of them may mean the difference between tragedy or tranquillity in the kitchen.

PREVENTION

Carelessness most often causes burn accidents. Prevent them by arranging your kitchen for safety. Cook on back burners whenever possible. Turn pot handles inward to keep them out of children's reach. Keep window curtains, hanging towels, and frilly aprons away from stove. See that stove and oven are free of all grease. Use pot holders to handle all hot plates and pans.

PREPAREDNESS

Be prepared for the sudden accident. Know the rules of first aid. If the burn is minor—that is, a reddening or a blistering of the skin—cover fine mesh gauze with pure petroleum jelly and place directly on the burn. A prepared sterile petrolatum gauze dressing may be used instead. Bandage firmly, but not so tightly as to affect circulation. If the burn seems deep or covers a wide area, do not touch it, but call a physician immediately.